TRANSITION MAGICIAN 2

More Strategies for Guiding Young Children in Early Childhood Programs

Mary Henthorne, Nola Larson, and Ruth Chvojicek
Illustrated by Mary Henthorne

Redleaf Press®
www.redleafpress.org
800-423-8309

Published by Redleaf Press
10 Yorkton Court
St. Paul, MN 55117
www.redleafpress.org

Illustrations by Mary Henthorne
Cover and book design by MacLean & Tuminelly
Printed in the United States of America

Library of Congress Cataloging-in-Publication Data
Henthorne, Mary, 1952–
     Transition magician 2 : more strategies for guiding young children in early childhood programs / by Mary Henthorne, Nola Larson, and Ruth Chvojicek ; illustrated by Mary Henthorne.
         p. cm.
     ISBN 978-1-884834-86-8 (pbk.)
         1. Early childhood education—Activity programs. I. Title: Transition magician two. II. Larson, Nola, 1941– III. Chvojicek, Ruth, 1956– IV. Title.

LB1139.35.A37 H45 2000
372.13—dc21   00-045741

Printed on acid-free paper

To Barbara Plum, our special friend who died June 22, 1997.
Our memory of Barb has been a constant inspiration
in writing this book.

She was a radiant Star, a caring Advocate,
a Teacher dedicated to her profession,
a Magician who journeyed with us in writing
Transition Magician,
and most of all,
a Friend who beautifully touched our lives.

Contents

Preface

Since the 1994 publication of *Transition Magician: Strategies for Guiding Young Children in Early Childhood Programs,* we have received very positive feedback from our readers and workshop participants. One participant commented, "I was so excited, I went home last night and planned exciting transitions for the next day. It was nice that I could do this without a lot of time and preparation." As we continue to work with teachers across the nation, we recognize that the need for transition activity ideas has not diminished. In fact, the need grows as agencies, centers, and classrooms enroll more children of varying ages (infants, toddlers, preschoolers, and schoolagers) and varying abilities (children with developmental disabilities or other exceptional needs) in inclusive programs. Managing a diverse group of challenging children seems to top the list of concerns. So in this book we will accommodate both children with disabilities and also toddlers.

Also new in this book is a teaching strategy we used in developing the transition activities. By adapting the concept of *emergent curriculum* (curriculum that *emerges* from children's life experience and interests), we developed *emergent transitions*—the idea of planning transitions based on a topic that interests your children and changing transitions as their needs, developmental abilities, and interests change.

We have written *Transition Magician 2* to address the concerns that you, the teachers and caregivers, have voiced to us since the publication of *Transition Magician.* We sincerely hope that this book will give you additional ideas that will make transitions a magical time for you and your children.

Suggestions for Using This Book

We have written *Transition Magician 2* to serve as a transition resource for early childhood teachers. This book includes transition activities and a planning format that will enable you to develop your own transition activities by using a webbing and brainstorming technique.

The first chapter, "The Magician's Plan," begins by summarizing concepts found in our first book, *Transition Magician.* These concepts laid the foundation for *Transition Magician 2,* and we thought it important to offer some grounding for those who have not read the first book.

"The Magician's Plan" continues by describing the three major concepts of this new book:

* Planning for Toddlers
* Planning for Children with Disabilities
* Planning for Emergent Transitions

"Planning for Toddlers" and "Planning for Children with Disabilities" provide background information and guidelines for working with these groups of children. We encourage you to read this information and incorporate the guidelines into transitions and other daily routines.

"Planning for Emergent Transitions" provides background information about emergent curriculum planning and how that can be applied to planning transitions. This discussion sets the stage for using the Magician's Maps in the rest of the book.

"Developing a Magician's Map" describes the steps that the reader can use to develop emergent-transition maps and activities. Five topics have been selected and transition activities developed to model the Magician's Map concept for you. These activities are, generally speaking, appropriate to use with all preschool children. However, we have used icons to indicate when an activity is particularly suited for toddlers or for children with disabilities. The Icon/Transition Strategy Chart, found in appendix H, will give you a quick overview of the Magician's Maps and transition activities found in this book.

Acknowledgments

A special thank you to our dear husbands, Jeff, John, and Ken, who were there for us while we wrote this book. Thanks to Ruth's children, Jenny and Ben, who helped their mom on this project.

For being receptive to our ideas and encouraging our work, we thank friends and early childhood professionals, especially the teaching staff of the Social Development Commission Head Start and its delegate agencies; Milwaukee Public Schools Head Start, Milwaukee, WI; all students past and present in the Child Care and Development Program at Western Wisconsin Technical College; and the staff of Western Wisconsin Technical College's Parent Child Center.

For review of content: Jenny Brunt, early childhood special education teacher, Cooperative Educational Service Agency #5; Ann Hollyfield and Fran Hast, Palo Alto, CA, authors of *Infant and Toddler Experiences;* Lilian Katz, Ph.D., professor emerita of early childhood education, University of Illinois, Champaign; Marcia Makowski, formerly an early exceptional educational needs program teacher and currently a kindergarten teacher, Onalaska School District, Onalaska, WI; Shirley Peterson, formerly a toddler teacher for New Morning Preschool and currently an early childhood consultant and toddler specialist, Madison, WI; and Sharlene Weibel, toddler teacher at the Parent Child Center, Western Wisconsin Technical College, La Crosse.

For typing our manuscript: Heidi Thompson.

For individual ideas: Marinella Pro and Kathy Hass.

Chapter 1: The Magician's Plan

Of all the daily routines and activities in an early childhood classroom, transitions are the most critical. How well you manage transitions with children sets the tone for the entire day. Appropriate transitions welcome children as they arrive, effortlessly connect daily activities, help keep children focused as they move through the day, and bid them a fond farewell so they're eager to return.

Summary of Transition Concepts

Planning transitions is a major concept in our book *Transition Magician*. This may not sound like a novel idea. However, it's surprising how many teachers overlook this simple step! Daily routines, whether in the toddler room or with preschoolers, will take place smoothly when you are prepared. In *Transition Magician* (Larson, Henthorne, and Plum, 1994), we based transition planning on our Triple-A approach to guiding young children—Anticipate, Act, Avert. Teachers *anticipate* by examining the classroom environment and the daily schedule, then *act* by making changes such as including transitions in the lesson plan, to *avert* potential behavior problems. We have included evaluation tools from *Transition Magician* in appendix C of this book because we believe observation and evaluation are essential steps toward improving transitions. A teacher's ability to plan effectively using the Triple-A approach also depends on a sound knowledge of child development and of age-appropriate expectations for children with varying abilities.

Readers of *Transition Magician* were given a "bag of tricks" that contained numerous transition activities along with directions for props they could make. The book identified eight critical kinds of transitions in the daily schedule:

★ **Routine Changes**—Changes in routine or activities, signaled with a sensory cue.

★ **Settlers**—Techniques used to gather children together and prepare and quiet them for the upcoming group time.

★ **Attention Grabbers**—Interesting objects or brief activities designed to get and focus children's attention.

★ **Stretchers**—Exercises that get children and staff moving and stretching.

★ **Extenders**—Activities that extend the time when you have a few minutes to fill or expand children's knowledge about a current or a previously learned topic.

★ **Magic Carpet Activities**—Learning activities done in a designated "magic carpet" place while waiting for others to finish a task.

★ **Magical Moments**—Times when a group of children are between activities, on the move, or out of the room.

★ **Excusers**—The methods used to dismiss children from a group time and transition them to another activity.

In *Transition Magician 2,* we have developed transition activities based on five open-ended topics. Each of these topics begins with a Magician's Map, a format we have used for brainstorming transition activities in the emergent curriculum. Within the structure of the map, we have organized the transition activities by the eight categories above. Each chapter is filled with all-new "bag of tricks" ideas to solve your transition challenges!

Plans for Toddlers on the Move

Amy's group of eight toddlers at Little Steps Child Care is about to go for a stroll in the neighborhood. Before they leave, the toys need to be picked up. As Amy hands a toy to one toddler she announces that it is time to pick up all the toys. Calmina, the assistant in the room, reinforces this by encouraging the toddlers in the opposite side of the room to begin picking up too. By now they have four toddlers picking up toys. Amy thinks, "Oh, this isn't so bad, we'll be on our way in no time." What neither she nor Cal realizes is that the other four toddlers just behind them are curiously taking the toys back off the shelves and engaging in more play. As Amy turns around and discovers what is happening, she thinks, "Perhaps this is going to take longer than I thought. Maybe we should just stay inside today."

Toddlers go through many routine transitions during their day. One of the more difficult is clean-up. Teachers may feel the desire to just leave the toys out, to pick them all up themselves, or as a last resort, to provide fewer toys for the toddlers so that clean-up is less overwhelming. As conscientious child care providers, we know that these are not the best options. What can Amy and Cal do to get through this routine change while involving the toddlers?

First, Amy and Cal need to *anticipate* that clean-up time will be a recurring problem. Expecting all toddlers to clean up the toys at the same time for more than a couple of minutes is not realistic. To do this they need to work cooperatively, and that is not a developmental skill that toddlers have accomplished yet. Although Amy and Cal may do the majority of the picking up, they should encourage the toddlers to do some, even if it's getting each two year old to put at least one toy back on the shelf. Toddlers are not purposely avoiding clean-up time, but their natural curiosity overrides the idea of putting away all those stimulating toys.

Next, Amy and Cal need to take *action* by establishing a plan to engage the toddlers in cleaning up the toys. One way to *avert* the problem is to make this routine a part of their play. A teacher walking through the room pulling a cardboard-box "wagon" and collecting the toys will motivate the toddlers to drop in their toys. By encouraging them to follow the box wagon, the teacher can lead the toddlers over to the shelves and conclude clean-up time by having them put a toy or two in the appropriate place. Amy and Cal need to model this and reinforce those who are complying. As the room becomes tidier, Amy and Cal can talk to the toddlers about their next activity, a stroll through the neighborhood. As Cal finishes clean-up, Amy can go with some of the toddlers to their cubbies to get their jackets. Taking this action will make the transition seamless, with no beginning or end in the flow of a playful day.

Toddlers thrive on repetition. It gives them a sense of security. Amy and Cal should repeat this type of transition as long as the toddlers show interest. The box wagon will become a natural part of their play. Placing the toys in the wagon and then putting them on the shelf will become a familiar and comfortable transition.

Truly, toddlerhood is a terrific time in children's lives. They are becoming more mobile and developing independence. Although they have a strong urge for worldly exploration, they still have that need to feel secure with the people who care for them. Toddlers need to know that you have provided a safe and predictable environment for them. Our goal as teachers is to maintain that sense of curiosity and allow them to explore their surroundings even during transitions. Use the following guidelines to ensure toddlers' safety, while engaging them in natural and meaningful transitions throughout their daily routines.

Guidelines for Successful Transitions with Toddlers

* Be sensitive to toddlers' need to feel secure in your environment. Greet them with tenderness as they arrive. Verbally and physically assure them that you are truly glad to see them. Have a favorite toy or object close at hand so you can involve them in enjoyable play as the parents leave. Encourage parents to bring "security items" such as blankets, pacifiers, or stuffed animals that will help the toddlers relax at naptime. At the end of the day, prepare the toddlers for the parents' return, gathering all those security items to be sent home for the night. Give the parents a record of their children's routines, such as when they slept, what they ate, and the number of diaper changes or successes on the potty chair.

* Identify necessary transitions for toddlers, including routines such as arrival and departure, diapering and toileting, eating, and naptime. Also consider the normal transitions in a child care setting like dressing for outdoor play, cleaning up, and gathering interested toddlers for a "drop and flop" time to read a story or sing some songs. Some of these transitions need to be done on an individual basis. Take advantage of this one-on-one time you have with each toddler. This type of transition gives you the

opportunity to converse quietly with the toddler, telling her what you are doing and showing your respect for her as an individual. These are excellent times to bond. Provide toys and other props that can be played with independently for the toddlers who are waiting for their special time with you. When the transition engages a group of toddlers, plan how you will motivate them, taking into consideration their interests, needs, and abilities. For example, if you have a group that likes music, sing with the toddlers as they transition.

★ Give one simple direction at a time when transitioning toddlers. Move with them, modeling what you expect them to do. As you carry out the transition, tell the toddlers what you are doing. Encourage them to join you. Reinforce them as they comply. Close to the end of the transition, talk to the toddlers about the fun activity that is to come.

★ Provide developmentally appropriate props for toddlers to manipulate during transitions that require waiting. Remember that toddlers are sensory learners. They like to fill and dump, push and pull, and stack. They explore materials using all their senses, turning an object around in their hands as they gaze at it, shaking it to make noise, squeezing and poking it, and mouthing it. Give each object the choke-tube test to ensure it is safe for toddlers. Remember to have enough props for each toddler to have one, because toddlers have difficulty sharing or waiting for their turn.

★ Observe toddlers and identify their interests as individuals and as a group. Plan transition activities that have a natural flow, that actively engage toddlers, and that motivate them to become involved. Once successful strategies are established, repeat them consistently. By doing and redoing, toddlers reinforce skills, develop autonomy, and grow in self-confidence.

★ Develop a "bag of tricks" to be used specifically during transitions that require waiting. One critical time is waiting for the parents to arrive at the end of the day. Often toddlers' interest in the toys they have been playing with all day is waning, and they are getting tired. Have a special bag or box of new and different props that can be taken out and then quickly put away when it's time to leave. It's very important for toddlers to enjoy these last minutes, so that they will be eager to return the next day.

Plans for Children with Disabilities

Children in a Head Start inclusive classroom eat lunch in the school's cafeteria. This means that Mrs. B and her assistant, Ginny, take fifteen children with varying abilities down the hall to a large, noisy lunchroom. As children finish their lunch, they go into an adjacent gymnasium with Mrs. B to wait for the rest of the group to finish lunch before returning to their classroom. One day, Jason, Audra, Kendall, and Shad are the first ones in the gym. Mrs. B tries to sing some songs while she is adjusting Audra's braces, but no one is listening. Within minutes, Kendall and Shad are running circles around Jason, the teacher, and Audra. What's more, Mrs. B fears these children will never settle down once they get back to their classroom.

There are times in your work with children that you simply need more hands—or a better plan. We teachers need to figure out ways to "work smarter, not harder." What can Mrs. B and Ginny do to ease the children's transition from the lunchroom to the classroom?

They can anticipate this challenging transition and make a plan. That plan includes a division of labor. The teachers take turns being responsible for the gym time. The assigned teacher writes out her plans for gym activities, complete with all the necessary equipment or materials, making sure the activities are appropriate for the children. She may have a felt-board box with familiar story pieces for Jason and Audra, who generally prefer quieter activities. The box frees her to be with Kendall and Shad, the more active ones, to oversee a beanbag-tossing game.

Regardless of children's varying abilities or challenging behaviors, our expectations for them must be appropriate to their developmental level. It is essential that we know and understand child development. Only then do we truly know what activities and experiences are appropriate for the children in our care.

Teachers can expect to see more inclusion of children with disabilities in their classrooms as lawmakers, parents, and educators recognize the value of placing children in the least restrictive environment. Research also shows that children with disabilities benefit from being with their typically developing peers. In order to provide the best services for children with specific challenges and disabilities, we need to learn more about the nature of each child's disability. In addition to children with developmental delays or physical disabilities, we may see children with attention deficit disorder (ADD) or attention deficit/hyperactivity disorder (ADHD), children with autism, children who have been traumatized by life events, or children with sensory integrative dysfunction. Some of these children have a very difficult time with change. Transitions will be their undoing if the teacher doesn't carefully plan the environment, the schedule, and transition times for them. For more information about specific disabilities mentioned above, refer to the teacher resources in appendix B.

Children are more alike than they are different. We find that many typically developing children display characteristics similar to the disorders mentioned above—but not to the same degree. The bottom line is that all children can benefit from carefully anticipated and planned transitions. The guidelines for improving transitions used in *Transition Magician 2* apply to all children regardless of their ability. However, some of those guidelines should be applied specifically and more intentionally to certain children in our care. The following guidelines apply to children with sensory, physical, and neurological dysfunctions. As always, keep in mind the child's strengths and interests when planning transitional activities.

Guidelines for Successful Transitions with Children with Disabilities

* Establish a consistent classroom routine. Any change in routines, especially for children with ADD/ADHD, can cause dramatic problems. Preview any change in activities for the child. For example, start your day by sharing a pictorial schedule and refer to it when children are about to make a transition. Establish rituals that children can count on.

* Provide a safe environment for children. A safe environment is one where there is space and time for children to be alone some of the time; where there is a consistent nurturing caregiver from day to day; and where classroom rules and expectations are clear and consistent.

* Control the level of stimulation by eliminating distractions, slowing down the activity, or using quiet activities. Children can benefit from signals that will help them slow down, such as a "stop-and-go wand" or a timer. Or they might need a quiet place or an individual space to calm down or to ease their tension.

* Establish the children's full attention before giving directions. Visual and auditory cues help attract and sustain their attention. When a child is tuning out, use the child's name along with a visual cue, such as a picture of the next activity mounted on a tongue depressor, to signal the transition. Help children plan what they are going to do next. If necessary, physically guide them to the next activity.

* Present tasks or situations in clear, small steps. Use a picture or a rebus (a chart using words and pictures) to outline what children are to do when they enter the classroom, or place footprints to show the path they are to take. Give one-, two-, or three-step directions. Be sure to check on progress before giving the next step.

* Present activities that are new and different. Use novel props that will grab children's attention, such as a puppet or a marionette. Change your tone of voice for different characters, or lower it to get children's attention. However, remember that children, especially if they have ADHD, can become overstimulated by too many props. Balance novelty with structure in your classroom.

* Anticipate times when children may become agitated, and use strategies to calm and soothe them. Sit or move closer to the child, play calming music during activities and center time, or provide headsets with the child's favorite soothing music. See appendix B for a list of music resources.

* Give children something to do while they wait. Many children with ADHD benefit from the soothing effect of an object they can hold and manipulate. During group time or when a child has to wait, provide a Koosh ball, a worry stone, or a stress-relief ball. This can actually increase a child's concentration. Some active children can focus on a quiet activity like story time if they are allowed to sit in a child-sized rocking chair at the back of the group.

* Build on the children's strengths. By discovering the children's interests and planning activities based on those interests, you will help them focus and stay on task. For example, a child may have a fascination for large

pieces of machinery after observing construction at a nearby construction site. Provide books and toys related to construction and large machinery.

★ Model appropriate behavior and social skills. Many children with ADD/ADHD and other disabilities are socially delayed. Many simply do not have the social skills to appropriately enter into a play situation. This is where you and the child's peers can model waiting, taking turns, sharing, saying thank you, and so on.

★ Be prepared to adapt activities for a child with a specific physical disability. For example, if a child in your class is blind or has a visual impairment, using a transition activity that relies on sight will exclude her. Instead, plan an activity that uses sound or touch.

★ Step back and look at the situation—your environment, daily schedule, and daily planning—from time to time. Use the evaluation tools in appendix C.

Plans for Emergent Transitions

The teachers of Changing Times preschool program have carefully planned out their year in regard to the topics they will teach children of varying ages and abilities, topics that have been successful in the past. Teachers have even planned transitions that can enhance the topics. They are feeling organized and confident that it will be a good year. But as the year begins, children aren't responding the way they have in the past. The teachers plow forward, assuring themselves that the children will adjust. After all, these plans have always worked before. One month into the year, the teachers gather for their second staff meeting. Attitudes are not as positive. Some of the following comments are heard: "How can I be so worn out after only one month?" "These children sure are giving me a lot of problems." "I don't have a very compliant group this year." " I feel like a referee, helping children engage in appropriate social play." "I can't seem to get the children's attention." "I can't wait until this year is over."

What can the teachers at Changing Times do to make this year more enjoyable and interesting for them and for the children in their program? While it appears that these teachers are taking all measures to have a successful year, they have not taken into consideration some important facts.

Teachers need to know the children in their care in order to plan appropriately. Bredekamp and Copple (1997) list three important kinds of information that professionals need when they make decisions about educating children:

1. General knowledge of child development and learning

2. Specific information about the strengths, interests, and needs of each individual child in the group

3. Knowledge of the social and cultural contexts in which these children live

The decisions teachers make about transitional activities, just like the decisions they make for curriculum planning, need to reflect that knowledge and information.

Guidelines for Successful Transitions

1. Plan and develop transitional activities that are appropriate for children's developmental abilities. For example, give toddlers only one task at a time, and closely guide them as they move from one place to another. For preschoolers who are visual learners, you will need to match a verbal cue with a visual prop in order to keep the child on task at clean-up time. Adapt the activities and directions to match children's abilities as they grow and develop more skills.

2. Plan and develop transitions that reflect the children's strengths and interests. In *Emergent Curriculum*, Jones and Nimmo (1994) define *emergent curriculum* as a planning process that emerges from children's daily lives and keeps their developing interests in mind. Just as children's abilities change, so do their interests. Tune in to children's interests—transitions that focus on the children's current interests can connect or bridge activities in the emergent curriculum.

3. Plan and develop transitional activities that reflect the cultural and social differences of the children in your care. For example, be respectful of cultural expectations about such things as separating from mom and dad or participating in self-help skills. Sing the clean-up song in Hmong or Spanish if that is the home language of children in your group. If a child is highly distractible and has difficulties entering the classroom, help that child focus and succeed by making a pictorial plan of the first three tasks she must do when she enters the classroom. Help children enter into play with others in socially acceptable ways. By anticipating children's needs and using your knowledge of development, you can help each child make successful transitions.

   When transitions are effective, children will "magically" move to the next daily routine without even recognizing what is happening. In other words, transitions are part of a seamless curriculum plan to ensure a smooth flow from one routine or activity to another. Imagine that you have been focusing on the topic of light and dark and you are about to transition your toddlers to the lunch table. Dim the lights and lead your group to the table with a flashlight guiding the way. What fun! The toddlers are engaged in the transition and are also learning about light and dark.

   As you prepare for seamless transitions,

   * Consider the developmental abilities and the varying needs of your children when choosing transitions.
   * Connect transitions with the curriculum for more incidental learning.
   * Choose broad topics so they can easily be adapted to the interests of all children.

* Change your transition techniques when they become ineffective.
* Brainstorm your transitions by developing a Magician's Map around a topic of interest to the children.

Developing a Magician's Map

Be a transition magician! By using a curriculum webbing strategy and brainstorming transitional activities, you can create what we call a Magician's Map—a collection of transition activities, based on the topic being discussed, that serve as links from one activity to another in the emergent curriculum. Following is a step-by-step approach for developing a Magician's Map and planning emergent transitions that speak to your children's interests. Use this approach individually or with teaching partners.

Steps to a Magician's Map

1. Observe your group of children to become aware of their interests and developmental abilities.

2. Based on your observations, decide on a topic. Plan your curriculum, and thus your transitions, by choosing open-ended topics that hold meaning and interest for the children. If the topic is open-ended, it provides more flexibility in designing transitional activities. For example, once a teacher brainstormed the topic *water* and planned many water activities for the children. Several children in her class vacationed in Florida and brought back seashells and pictures of sea life that prompted a new interest in the water topic.

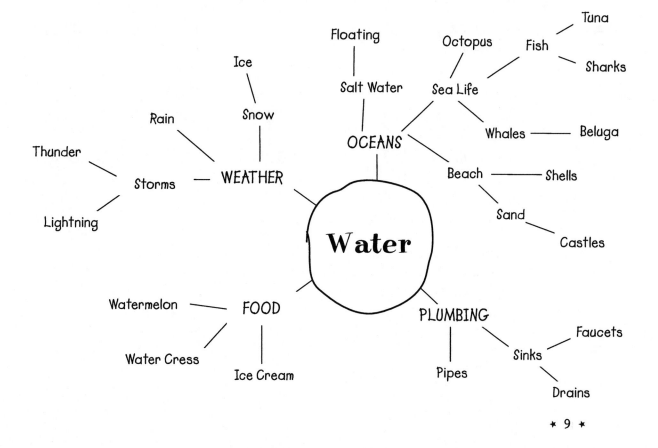

3. Web or brainstorm the topic, for example, sea life. Involve children in the brainstorming to get their ideas about what they enjoy doing.

4. Based on what you know about your children, the classroom environment, and the daily schedule, decide which types of transitions you should use throughout the day (routine changes, settlers, attention grabbers, stretchers, extenders, Magic Carpet activities, Magical Moments, or excusers). For example, if you are working with toddlers, you may not have group times with all children engaged in the same activity at the same time. Therefore, you may not need to plan settlers or excusers. If you have several children who have difficulty getting to the next activity, you might focus particularly on routine changes or attention grabbers.

5. Using the master web reproduced below (you may photocopy the full-size version in appendix D), plan transition activities based on the topic you've chosen, in the categories that are important in your day. See the sea-life web on the following page for an example.

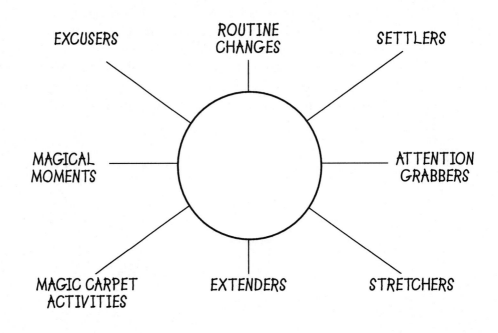

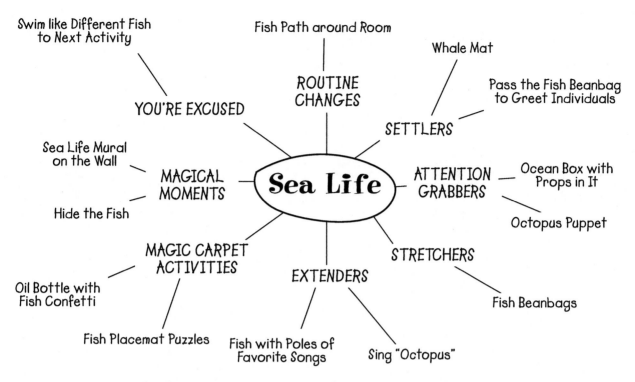

6. Plan how you are going to use these transitions to bridge one routine or activity to the next.

Consider what props you have or will need to make in order to implement the transitions. Some props can be used in multiple ways; for example, in the sea-life web, Fish Beanbags are used as both settler and stretcher. This makes efficient use of your time and materials. In the next chapters of *Transition Magician 2,* we have chosen five open-ended topics to give you a start in developing your own maps. Each topic begins with a Magician's Map. Each map shows transition activities around a given topic, organized into the eight types of transitions. The activities include the transition strategy, variations (describing different types of transitions that can be accomplished with the same prop), materials, and directions for making the props.

Use the examples in these chapters to help you develop your own emergent transitions. Many of the following transition activities can be adapted for use with your own topics. Our hope is that you continue this process with new topics that interest your children and meet their needs. You, too, can become a transition magician!

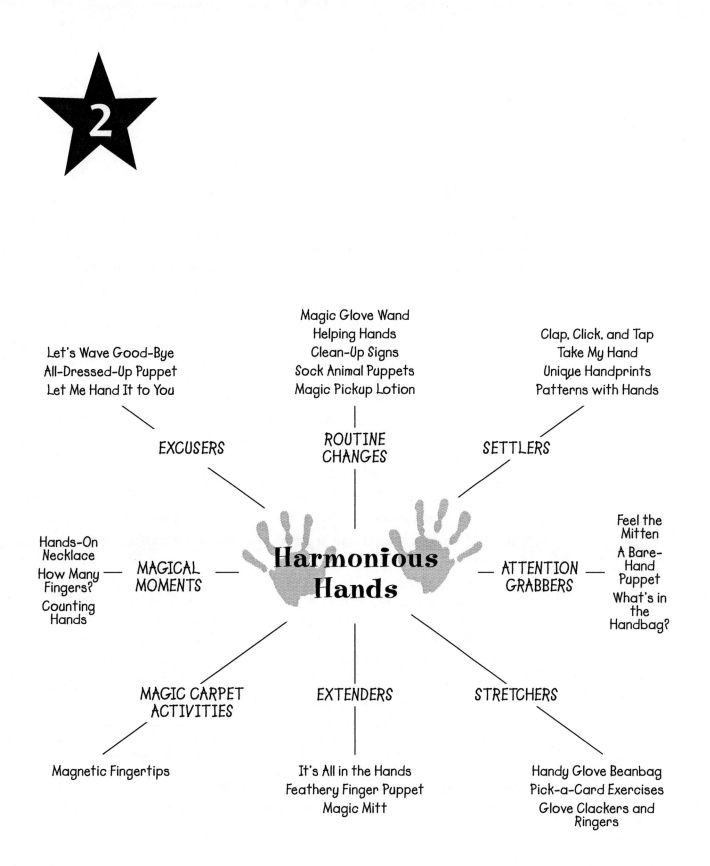

2

Magic Glove Wand
Helping Hands
Clean-Up Signs
Sock Animal Puppets
Magic Pickup Lotion

Let's Wave Good-Bye
All-Dressed-Up Puppet
Let Me Hand It to You

Clap, Click, and Tap
Take My Hand
Unique Handprints
Patterns with Hands

EXCUSERS

ROUTINE
CHANGES

SETTLERS

Hands-On
Necklace
How Many
Fingers?
Counting
Hands

MAGICAL
MOMENTS

Harmonious
Hands

ATTENTION
GRABBERS

Feel the
Mitten
A Bare-
Hand
Puppet
What's in
the
Handbag?

MAGIC CARPET
ACTIVITIES

EXTENDERS

STRETCHERS

Magnetic Fingertips

It's All in the Hands
Feathery Finger Puppet
Magic Mitt

Handy Glove Beanbag
Pick-a-Card Exercises
Glove Clackers and
Ringers

Magic Glove Wand

Transition Strategy

The Magic Glove Wand has diverse uses for routine changes. It can be used, for example, to show the number of minutes left before cleaning up, as a pointer to the toys that need to be put away, or as an indicator of the number of toys each child should pick up. Because each of the fingers has Velcro fastener stripping, a given number of them can be left up or bent down. To give a warning right before clean-up, put three fingers up on the glove wand and ask children how many more minutes they have to play. Then, at the end of the three minutes, tell the children it's time to clean up. When you see children putting away the toys, reinforce them by giving the thumbs-up signal with the wand. Point to the area that they will be going to after all the toys are put away. Often children who resist the direction of the teacher will respond better when you guide them more creatively with a prop such as this glove wand.

Variations

* **Settler:** Wave to the children with the wand as they come to group time. Sing your favorite greeting song at the same time.

* **Attention Grabber:** Stick a secret note on the Velcro stripping of the glove.

* **Stretcher:** One red and one green glove could be used to start and stop movement as the children stretch.

* **Extender:** Keep one or two Magic Glove Wands handy during group time. Have the children shut their eyes, and put a number of fingers up on the wand. Say this little chant to cue the children to open their eyes, "Handy, dandy look at me. How many fingers do you see?" Have the children count the fingers and respond to the question.

Handy Dandy – (tune: The Universal Chant)

Han-dy dan-dy look at me. How ma-ny fin-gers do you see?

★ **Magical Moment:** Use the glove wand to point to various parts of the body. Choose a child to show you one way that he can move a body part. Have the children move their own body part in that way. When the wand goes up in the air, it's time to stop.

Materials

Stretchy one-size-fits-all knitted glove
Polyester fiber stuffing
9-inch dowel or chopstick
Sandpaper
Fabric glue or hot-glue gun
5 small pieces hooked fastener stripping
Optional: ⅛-inch or ¼-inch satin ribbon (two or three
   colors)—approximately 2-foot lengths of each color

Directions

1. Sand a dowel so it is smooth, especially one end (if you use a chopstick you can omit this step).

2. Fill a stretchy glove sparingly with stuffing (full enough to give it form, but loose enough so the fingers can still bend easily).

3. Cover 1 inch of one end of the dowel with glue and insert approximately 2 inches into the stuffing in the glove.

4. Squeeze the stuffing around the stick to secure it.

5. Close and glue the opening of the glove around the stick.

6. Glue a small piece of the hooked Velcro stripping to the tip of each finger. The hooks of the Velcro will catch on the loops in the knitted glove.

7. To add color, tie a bow of two or three colors of ribbon around the stick at the base of the glove. This is optional.

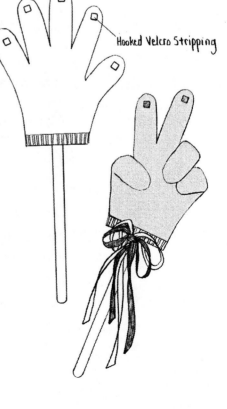

Hooked Velcro Stripping

Helping Hands

Transition Strategy

Cleaning up after playtime goes more smoothly if children have some direction or symbol indicating areas that need tidying. Cut out large hands from foam-rubber placemats and store them in a Helping Hands box. At the beginning of clean-up time, take these large hands from the box and place them in or near the areas in the room that need to be tidied. After the children have cleaned up the toys they were playing with, tell them to find a Helping Hand and pick up the toys in that area. Some areas that often need extra work include the blocks, dramatic play, and art center. Consider having children place the Helping Hands around the room in areas they think need cleaning. This helps children focus on the transition and gives them a sense of responsibility. After that area is clean, have the children take the Helping Hands and place them in the box. Look around the room for any other Helping Hands. If none are found, the children may go to the next activity or routine.

Materials

4–5 colorful foam-rubber placemats (found in the kitchen area of most stores)

Large hand stencil (draw a hand that is approximately the size of the placemat or 8 by 10 inches)

Scissors

Box with cover (large enough to place your Helping Hands in)

Printed Con-Tact paper

Black permanent marker

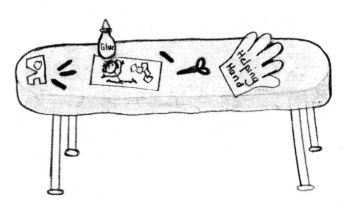

Directions

1. On the back side of the foam rubber placemats, trace the hand stencil.

2. Cut them out and print "Helping Hand" on each one with a permanent marker.

3. Cover a box that fits the hands with colorful Con-Tact paper.

4. Trace some handprints on the box and write "Helping Hands" on the cover with permanent marker.

Clean-Up Signs

Transition Strategy

It is beneficial for children to learn various forms of communication. One of the most intriguing forms is American Sign Language (ASL). Teach children the sign for *clean up.* Move around the room as children play, signaling clean-up time by using the sign. Encourage the children to pass the message by signing to their friends. Children feel quite special when they have learned this and can respond without your even having to use your voice. You may also want to teach them some reinforcement signs such as *good, thumbs-up,* and *clapping.*

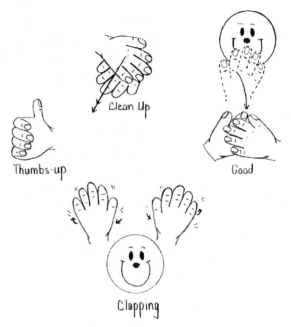

Variation

★ **Extender:** Teach children other basic signs for your daily routines, such as *toilet, eat, rest, outside, inside, story,* and *singing.* Now you will be able to sign what they will be doing after they are done cleaning up, and you just may have a quieter classroom because of it!

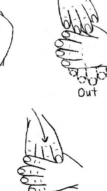

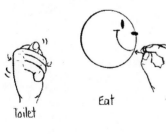

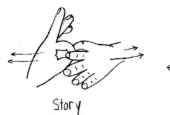

Sock Animal Puppets

Transition Strategy

Children love puppets and will listen to everything they have to say. When it's time to change activities, place this version of a sock puppet and paper animal on your arm to talk with the children and announce "clean-up time" or "a few more minutes left to play," and they will follow the puppet like it's the Pied Piper. Refer to the illustrations for an example of an animal to make.

Variations

★ **Attention Grabber:** Use a puppet to tell children what's happening for the day or what's new in the center area. They will listen with rapture as a spider or turtle tells them what's happening—even children who have a hard time sitting or listening.

★ **Excuser:** The puppet can announce who is excused to wash hands for lunch or get their coats on to go outside. For fun, give children turns holding the puppet.

Materials

Poster board
Construction paper
Markers
One light-colored sock
Clear Con-Tact paper

Directions

1. Refer to the illustration for a sample animal pattern. Draw the body of an animal shape on colored poster board. Cut out.

2. Cover entire puppet with clear Con-Tact paper.

3. Cut hole out of puppet where head should be.

4. Place sock over hand. Tuck the sock in between fingers and thumb for the mouth.

5. Using permanent marker, draw eyes and nose in appropriate places. Open and close hand to make puppet mouth move.

6. To use, pull the sock over your hand, then slip your hand through the opening for the puppet's head.

ROUTINE
CHANGE

Magic Pickup Lotion

Transition Strategy

Clean-up time is often a challenging time in the daily schedule. Make it intriguing for children by introducing Magic Pickup Lotion. Just the idea that rubbing a little glitter lotion on their hands will help them pick up the blocks faster or hang up the dramatic play clothes makes clean-up time fun. It's the distraction of the lotion that helps them move out of one activity into the next. As with many of the transition ideas in this book, when the novelty wears off, put the lotion away for a while and reintroduce it later.

Variation

★ **Settler:** As the children come to circle, give them a little "quiet lotion" to rub on their hands while they wait. For children who have attention deficits, this is an excellent way to keep their hands busy. It's calming, too.

Materials

Little plastic bottles—use lotion bottles from your stay at a motel, or obtain from Discount School Supplies (see Teacher Resources in appendix B)
Baby lotion
Glitter—purchase "plastic" glitter from the Discount School Supplies catalog (see appendix B)

Directions

1. Fill small plastic bottle with baby lotion.

2. Add a pinch of glitter and shake bottle.

3. Use a special sticker to label it "Magic Pickup Lotion."

Note: Use a mild lotion and be aware of children who might be sensitive to perfumes and other ingredients.

Clap, Click, and Tap

Special Needs

Toddler

Transition Strategy

After a few children finish their tasks and come to group time, begin interaction with them. Getting the children involved helps them settle down and encourages the rest of the children to arrive more quickly. Here is an easy and fun little tune for hand actions.

"Clapping, Click, Tapping, Quick" (tune: "Where is Thumbkin?")
Clapping, clapping, clapping, clapping.
Click, click, click, click, click, click.
Tapping, tapping, tapping, tapping, tapping, tapping.
Fold them quick, fold them quick.

These actions are definitely for older preschoolers. Be creative in the actions you choose according to the developmental abilities of the children you are working with. Using the same tune, sing the following song with toddlers:

"Put Your Hands" (tune: "Where is Thumbkin?")
Put your hands on your knees.
On your toes, on your toes.
Put your hands on your head.
On your nose, on your nose.

Some children learn songs more easily with a visual cue. Take pictures of children as they do the actions to these songs. Enlarge the photos to 8 by 10 inches on a color copier. Insert the enlarged photos into page protectors on an accordion board. (See page 109 for directions for making an Accordion Photo Board with page protectors.)

Variations

★ **Extender:** Once the children are familiar with this song, encourage them to make up new hand actions. Use these new verses while children are waiting for the next activity or routine to start.

★ **Magical Moment:** Hang the accordion board on the wall in front of the potty chairs. Toddlers can do the song while sitting on their chairs.

Materials

For making the
 photo prompt:
Camera with film
Color copier
Accordion Photo
 Board

SETTLER

Take My Hand

Transition Strategy

Toddlers feel safe and secure when you are clutching their hands. As you invite one or more to a "drop and flop" activity, hold out your hands and lovingly guide them to that cozy area for quiet interaction. While you are still holding hands, sit down and help them settle in for some quality time with you. If more than one toddler wants to join you, have the second child take your other hand or the hand of his friend as you lead the way. Preschoolers who have difficulty getting to the requested destination during a transition benefit from this Take My Hand activity.

Variations

* **Routine Change:** Guide a toddler during clean-up time by holding his hand with one of your hands—and carrying a toy to the shelves with your other hand.

* **Stretcher:** Toddlers like to hold hands with you as they move to music.

* **Excuser:** After you have finished your "drop and flop" activity, take toddlers gently by the hand one more time and walk to the next routine or area. As you walk with the toddler, talk about what is going to happen next.

★ 21 ★

SETTLER

Unique Handprints

Transition Strategy

Have each child in your group make a handprint to show off her uniqueness. Put the child's name on it and use it as an attendance marker. When setting up your group area each day, lay the children's handprints to show where you would like them to sit. As they come to group time, have them find their handprints, pick them up, place them in the attendance container marked "here," and then sit on their space. As they are going through this process, clap and cheer for them, acknowledging that you are glad to see each child. Encourage the other children to greet all their friends in the same manner.

There are various reasons for seating children in specific places. Children who have a hearing disability should be placed directly in front of you so they can see your signs and read your lips. Children who have a difficult time maintaining attention should be placed close to you so you can tactilely reinforce them. Place children who have behavior problems between two assertive, well-behaved children to model appropriateness. Children who have a visual disability should be positioned in a well-lighted area where there is no glare from the lights on books.

Variations

★ **Stretcher:** Pick a handprint out of the "here" container. Let that child choose an action to do with her hands. Encourage the rest of the children to do the action too.

★ **Extender:** If you need to extend your group time, pick a handprint out of the container, showing children only the back . Give clues about the child whose handprint you have, until the group identifies that child. Choose another handprint and keep the guessing game going as long as needed. This is an excellent opportunity to make supportive comments about each child as an individual.

★ **Extender:** Decorate another container and write "gone." Then you can talk with the children about who is gone that day and how you miss them. Place their names in the "gone" container.

★ **Magical Moment:** Take the container with handprints to where children are waiting for the bus or for lunch to be served. Draw a handprint out and encourage that child to share something special about himself or his family.

★ **Excuser:** Use the handprints to excuse children from group time. Pull out a handprint and show it to the group. Ask the children to identify the name or the print, helping as necessary. Then excuse that child to go to the next activity or routine.

Materials

Poster board
Fingerpaint—skin tones are one idea, but you can use any color
Large paintbrush
Tongue depressors
Glue
Scissors
Clear Con-Tact paper or laminating film
Black water-base marker
Container such as box, basket, or can
Rubber cement
Photos of individual children (optional)

Directions

1. Brush fingerpaint on each child's hands and have her press her painted hands onto a piece of poster board.

2. Place the wet handprints aside and, on an extra sheet of paper (cut to cover the container), have the child print off as much excess paint as possible. Wash the child's hands.

3. After the handprints are dry, cut around them and write the child's name on them. (If you have children who are not able to recognize their own handprints or names, include a small photo on the handprints.)

4. Glue a tongue depressor on the back of the handprints to create a handle. Cover both sides of the handprints with clear Con-Tact paper and cut around the edge, leaving a ¼-inch lip (or laminate before attaching the tongue depressor).

5. Use rubber cement to adhere the sheet of paper that was created in step 2 to a container. Write "here" on it, and cover with clear Con-Tact paper.

Patterns with Hands

Transition Strategy

Many teachers of older preschoolers and kindergartners work with children on patterning. This activity does just that through the use of hand actions. As the children begin to gather for group time, begin some *ababab* hand patterns of opposite positions. For example, model opening and shutting the hands repeatedly while chanting the actions, and encourage the children to imitate the pattern with their hands. After everyone has done this pattern of opening and shutting for about half a minute, change the *ababab* pattern by repeatedly placing your hands near your body and then far away. Encourage the children to follow along as you model the changes. Continue "Patterns with Hands" until all the children have arrived at group time and settled. Some other hand patterns are

open	shut	high	low
near	far	out	in
left	right	apart	together
in front	behind	over	under

After the children become familiar with the activity, let them choose some hand patterns. Do each child's pattern until another child joins the group. Then let the joining child choose the next pattern. When all the children have gathered, do the last pattern. Slow the rate, chant more quietly, and choose a position that will get the children's hands into their laps. If the children get really good at the *ab* patterns, move on to *abc* patterns.

Variations

* **Extender:** At group times, chanting and hand patterning continue until the next activity or routine is ready to begin.

* **Magical Moment:** Make patterns while children are waiting for their turn in the bathroom or for the bus to arrive.

Feel the Mitten

Transition Strategy

It's amazing what you can do with one mitten to grab children's attention. Into any adult-size mitten, insert an object that pertains to your topic or is somewhat familiar to the children. As they arrive at group time, have them feel the outside of the mitten with their hands to help them guess what's inside. Encourage preschoolers to describe what they feel. Have them tell you if it is hard or soft, big or little, bumpy or smooth, and so on. When all children are settled and you have their attention, restate some of the guesses. Choose a child to pull the object out of the mitten, and proceed to talk about it. Feel the Mitten is a perfect lead into the topic being discussed.

During a "drop and flop" time, toddlers will feel the mitten for a short time, and then they will want to pull the object out to see what it is. They'll enjoy putting it back in the mitten and taking it out again . . . and again . . . and again. You can also play object-permanence games, which teach toddlers that an object is still there even if they can't see it. Insert a favorite toy and then ask the toddlers, "Where is the red block? Find the red block." If they don't know, show them. Try again. When they find the block, cheer for them!

Feel the Mitten is a particularly good activity for children who have a visual disability. Having a real object for them to feel as you label the item and discuss the texture allows them to learn about the world around them through the sense of touch.

Variations

* **Extender:** Have the children shut their eyes. Insert into the mitten an object that you've been using during group time. Have them open their eyes and pass the mitten around. After all the children have had a chance to feel the mitten and make some guesses, pull the object out to see if it has been guessed. Repeat the guessing game with other objects as long as necessary.

* **Magical Moment:** Feel the Mitten is sure to make waiting time pass quickly if you bring the mitten and some objects along.

A Bare-Hand Puppet

Transition Strategy

Make a fist with your thumb pointing up and touching the side of your pointer finger. Tip your fist down so your thumb is horizontal. Can you see a mouth right above the thumb? Roll the tip of your thumb down on your pointer to make it look like your fist is talking. Purchase some adhesive wiggly eyes and stick them on your hand right below the pointer knuckle. Other options are to use marker or pen to draw eyes right on your hand, or on small sticky dots. Now you have a Bare-Hand Puppet! When you need to get children focused on you, have your puppet make some attention-grabbing statements like "Hear ye, hear ye" or "Good morning all!" Have the puppet whisper in your ear. Children will strain to hear what it is saying. A Bare-Hand Puppet is a good transitional activity for both toddlers and preschoolers.

Note: Consider alternatives for wiggly eyes with toddlers, as they might pick the eyes off and put them in their mouths. The marker or sticker eyes are best for them.

Variations

*   **Stretcher:** Use Bare-Hand Puppets to give directions for various activities.

*   **Extender:** Have the Bare-Hand Puppet request songs or finger plays.

*   **Magical Moment:** Bare-Hand Puppets go right with you for Magical Moment transitions.

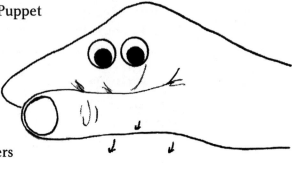

*   **Excuser:** Let the Bare-Hand Puppet excuse children from a group time or encourage toddlers to come for a diaper change.

Materials

Wiggly eyes, marker or pen, or small sticky dots

What's in the Handbag?

Toddler

Transition Strategy

A "handbag" (colorful and unusual purse, or a canvas bag decorated with hand-prints) will grab children's attention. Fill your handbag with props for the day. Open the bag and feel what's inside. Give children clues about what you are feeling. After someone has guessed an item in the handbag, pull out the item and talk about what it is and how it relates to your topic. Proceed with your lesson using that prop. As group time progresses, go back to your handbag and pull new props out as you get to each activity— the storybook you are going to read, the props to the song, and finally a wand to excuse children. Going back to the bag for each new prop renews children's interest throughout the group time.

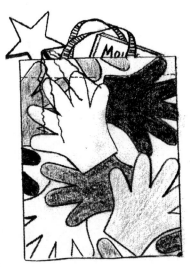

Variations

* **Settler:** As children come over to settle for group time, have children find their individual sitting space by placing a stick puppet or other item they have made on it. Greet children individually as you have them put their puppets in the handbag. At the end of group time pull the puppets out one at a time to excuse children.

* **Stretcher:** Insert some cards with pictures of exercises in the bag. Have children draw a card and do that exercise as a stretcher during group time.

* **Extender:** Keep some props for children's favorite songs in the bag to use when you need an extender for group time.

* **Magical Moment:** Use the handbag to play object-permanence games with toddlers during those Magical Moments. Hide an age-appropriate toy and see if they can find it.

Materials

Purchased handbag or purse—the more unusual the better
OR
Purchased canvas bag and decorating materials such as acrylic paints, markers, fabric paint, hand appliques, and iron

Directions

Decorate the canvas bag by having children make handprints with acrylic paint, tracing their hands with pencil and then going over the prints with permanent marker or fabric paint, or ironing on "hand" appliques.

STRETCHER

Handy Glove Beanbag

Special Needs

Transition Strategy

Give each child a Handy Glove Beanbag to shake, position, or manipulate to get those wiggles out. Have the children place beanbags on various parts of their bodies. Play a beanbag recording so children can move beanbags to music. Two good recordings are *Bean Bag Activities and Coordination Skills for Early Childhood* by Georgiana Stewart and *Me and My Bean Bag* by The Learning Station (1988). These recordings give directions on how children should manipulate the beanbag. Chant the following rhyme as you move: "Shake it high, shake it low, or shake it now as around you go."

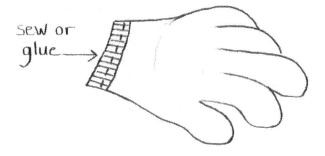
sew or glue →

Variations

★ **Settler:** Gently toss Handy Glove Beanbags to children as they come to group time and settle in for learning. Greet them individually as they catch the bags.

★ **Extender:** Play a passing game (found on the above recordings) with one beanbag to extend group time.

★ **Magic Carpet Activity:** Children can toss beanbags into a box during Magic Carpet activity time.

★ **Magical Moment:** Handy Glove Beanbags make excellent sensory props for children with disabilities during a Magical Moment.

★ **Excuser:** Have the children pass the beanbag from one to another as they are excused from group time.

Materials

Stretchy glove (one size fits all)—one per child
Aquarium rocks or pea gravel
Washable glue or sewing machine

Directions

1. Fill a stretchy glove approximately ¾ full with aquarium rocks.

2. Either glue the opening (at the wrist) with washable glue or sew the opening closed on a machine. Note: Beanbags can be washed and dried. Sewing is the safest method if you intend to wash and dry beanbags.

STRETCHER

Pick-a-Card Exercises

Transition Strategy

Make a deck of picture-and-word cards describing various hand actions. When making your cards, consider what your group of children can do with their hands. Spread your deck of cards and choose a child to come up and draw a card. Have the child show the card to the rest of the group and announce what the action will be (assist with identification if necessary). Have another child show a number from one to ten with fingers to tell the group how many times to repeat the action. Listed below are some actions to get you started:

clapping	clicking	waving
twirling	tapping	touching toes
rolling	clenching	folding

For toddlers, choose some of the simplest hand actions. Model and manipulate their hands to teach them various actions.

Materials

Poster board
Skin-tone and black water-base markers
Scissors
Pencil
Clear Con-Tact paper
Solid or printed Con-Tact paper

Directions

1. Cut several cards out of poster board, making them approximately 5 by 7 inches.

2. Draw and color various hand actions on the cards with different skin-tone markers.

3. Label the action on each card.

4. Lay the cards face down on a piece of clear Con-Tact paper, allowing approximately ½ inch between cards.

5. Lay a sheet of solid or printed Con-Tact paper over the backs of the cards.

6. Cut the cards out, leaving a lip of Con-Tact paper around the edges.

Modification

Instead of drawing hand actions, take photos of children doing the actions. Mount them on the poster board cards and cover with Con-Tact paper as in the directions above.

Glove Clackers and Ringers

Special Needs

Toddler

Transition Strategy

What fun children will have doing this stretching activity! Sew buttons and bells on gloves for children to wear so they can clack and ring to their favorite music. This is perfect for sensory learners and for children who need to move frequently. Hap Palmer's recording *Movin'* (1973) is an excellent choice of music, because it is all instrumental with various tempos. Note: If you have children who still put objects in their mouths, you might want to reconsider this activity.

You can use Glove Clackers and Ringers with toddlers if you sew the toys securely and watch the toddlers carefully. They will enjoy this musical activity.

Materials

Gloves—one or two one-size-fits-all stretch gloves for each child
Large, colorful plastic buttons
Jingle bells, approximately ¾-inch size
Heavy-duty thread
Needle
Scissors

Directions

1. Sew buttons on the inside tips of each finger and thumb of each glove. Use heavy-duty thread to make sure they will not fall off.

2. Sew three or four bells around the wristband of each glove. Tug on these after they are sewn to assure they can not be pulled off.

3. Alternately, make two gloves for each child—one with bells and the other with buttons. The bells can be sewn on the fingertips with this variation. Children can wear both gloves and alternate between sounds. Or sew buttons on the thumb and index finger and bells on the remaining fingers. With this type of glove, children will clack the buttons together and ring the bells at the same time.

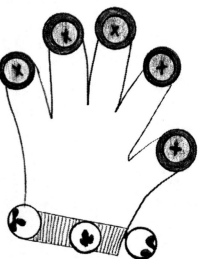

EXTENDER

It's All in the Hands

Transition Strategy

This activity is a favorite with preschoolers, because everyone's hands get to be busy. Choose a child to come to the center of the circle of children and cover his eyes. Then give a child sitting in the circle a novelty ring to wear, such as one with a plastic spider on it. Have all the children in the circle put their hands behind their backs. After everyone is ready, sing the following song:

"Who Has It" (tune: "Row, Row, Row Your Boat")
Who has the special ring hidden on their hand?
Can you guess who has the ring hidden on their hand?

After the song is sung the child in the middle uncovers his eyes. Give him three guesses to find the child with the ring. If the child doesn't correctly guess, the child with the ring shows the ring and then comes to the middle of the circle. The game starts all over again. Keep playing until it is time to move on to the next activity. If you have children who have difficulty sitting for a long time, consider choosing them early in the game. Also, as you sit down, position yourself close to such children so you can help them stay on task.

The ring can also be passed from child to child as the song is sung. When the song ends, the children stop passing the ring. Then the child in the middle can open his eyes and begin guessing.

Variations

★ **Routine Change:** At clean-up time during routine changes, give each child a spider ring. Tell him this is his "tidy bug" to help him pick up the toys. When he is done, have him come to the next activity. While he is waiting for the rest of the children to arrive, sing "The Itsy-Bitsy Spider" and do the hand actions. Collect the rings before you continue with group.

★ **Magic Carpet Activity:** Have some extra spider rings hidden in a small tub of sand. During Magic Carpet activities, children can use their hands to search for the spiders.

★ **Magical Moment:** Take a novelty ring along for a Magical Moment such as waiting for the bus. Have children cover their eyes. You or a child hides the ring in the area so it is slightly visible. When it's hidden, have the children open their eyes and look around for the ring while they remain sitting. When they spy the ring, have them start clapping their hands, or if the children need to be quiet, have them clap in sign language (see page 17). When most of the children are clapping, choose one child to get the ring.

★ **Excuser:** To end group time, have the children pass the ring around the circle. As each child passes the ring, she may be excused to the next routine or activity.

EXTENDER

Feathery Finger Puppet

Transition Strategy

This Feathery Finger Puppet is good for extending activities because you can keep it close at hand in case you have a short amount of time to wait before the next activity or routine begins. Use this puppet to talk with the children, choose songs to sing, tell stories, and hide and find. It is small and visually appealing and can be used in various ways. This puppet's hair made out of a feather boa is its most enticing feature, however, and for this reason, you will want to designate it as a "teacher puppet" with toddlers who still like to put objects in their mouths. Let the toddlers feel the hair, blow it, and watch the puppet as you manipulate it. Rub the toddlers' arms, necks, and cheeks with it. As for preschoolers, let them handle the puppet under your guidance. It's so easy to assemble that you might want to make a whole handful of Feathery Finger Puppets.

Variations

* **Settler:** This puppet can greet toddlers as they arrive at the center or preschoolers as they settle in for group time.

* **Attention Grabber:** Hide one puppet on each hand behind your back and have the children encourage them to come out.

* **Stretcher:** Stretching with the puppet is very enjoyable as the feathery hair blows and bobs in the air.

* **Magical Moment:** Use your Feathery Finger Puppet to talk with toddlers as they sit on the potty chair.

* **Excuser:** Have this puppet excuse the children, lead the way to the bus, and give the preschoolers one last tickle as they leave for the day.

Materials

Fabric that doesn't fray such as felt, blanket fabric (polar fleece), or looped Velcro fabric (use your scraps for this puppet)
Sewing machine
1-inch feather boa—the downy type purchased at craft or fabric stores
¼-inch pom-poms
Wiggly eyes (optional)
Black permanent marker, thin tipped
Fabric glue
Scissors
Pattern—see page 199

Directions

1. Photocopy or trace the actual-size pattern and cut it out.

2. With the fabric folded, right sides together, trace the pattern on the fabric and cut out. Or, if your fabric is thick, trace two sides of the pattern on the fabric and cut them out. You now have two pieces.

3. Lay the pieces right sides together and sew, leaving the bottom open.

4. Clip the seam around the curves and then turn the puppet right side out.

5. Glue two ¼-inch pom-poms close together near the top of the head.

6. Glue wiggly eyes on top of the pom-poms (optional).

7. Cut off approximately 1 inch of boa and pull away any loose down.

8. Glue the 1-inch strip of boa right above the eyes and down the back.

9. Draw a smile below the eyes with a black permanent marker.

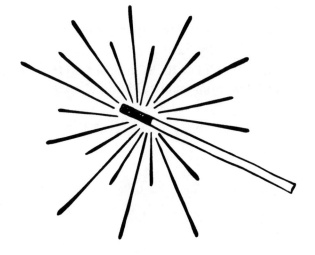

Magic Mitt

Transition Strategy

A Magic Mitt can be made from looped Velcro fastener fabric. Many types of lightweight material can be attached to the mitt with a small piece of Velcro fastener stripping. This mitt can act as a puppet to talk with the children or as a mini-Velcro board to tell stories, sing songs, or chant fingerplays. Keep it handy for group time. The Magic Mitt is also fun to use with toddlers during a "drop and flop" activity. They love taking the pieces off and putting them back on. Or, simply use an animal oven mitt or a child's bath mitt with a clever shape. These are perfect for toddlers because they have no loose pieces and are washable. Here are some ideas for the Magic Mitt:

"Away Up High in an Apple Tree"—Make the mitt in the shape of a tree from stiffened felt, heavy-weight interfacing, or milk filters from a farm-supply store; add apples made from red pom-poms.

"There Were Ten in the Bed"—Make "bears" from sheets of small decorative notepads, and a blanket from stiffened felt, heavy interfacing, or milk filters.

"Spot" books—Make doggy ears, tongue, and spots from felt, and eyes and nose from pom-poms.

"Take It Off, Put It On" toddler game—Cut shapes familiar and of interest to toddlers from foam-rubber place mats.

Variations

★ **Magic Carpet Activity:** Allow the children to manipulate the mitt and pieces during Magic Carpet time.

★ **Magical Moment:** Take the mitt along so children can sing songs or do finger plays while they wait for the bus or for their turn in the bathroom.

Materials

Looped Velcro fabric—a piece approximately 12 by 9 inches
Mitt pattern—see page 200
Sewing machine and thread
Scissors
Velcro stripping—approximately a 1-inch square per piece
Optional: Milk filters (white disks similar to interfacing, used in large milk
        tanks)—purchased at farm supply stores
      Stiffened felt (pennant fabric)—purchased at some craft stores
      Interfacing (the stiffest and heaviest weight)—purchased at
        fabric stores
      Decorative notepads (laminate or cover these with clear Con-Tact
        paper)—purchased at school supply stores
      Pom-poms—purchased at craft stores
      Felt—purchased at craft or fabric stores
      Foam-rubber place mats—purchased at discount stores

Directions

1. Draw two mitten shapes (minus the thumb) on the back of the looped Velcro fabric to fit your hand, or use the pattern on page 200.

2. Cut and place pieces front sides together.

3. Sew a seam around the mitt leaving the bottom open. Double-stitch ends.

4. Clip around the curves.

5. Turn so that front side is out.

6. Attach Velcro stripping to the backs of materials to be used with the Magic Mitt.

Magnetic Fingertips

Transition Strategy

Watch the magnetic pieces move in all directions! Children put on a glove with small magnets glued to each fingertip, then rub their fingertips along the sides of a bottle filled with baby oil and small magnetic items. Because the baby oil is clear, the children will be able to see the magnetic items move toward the magnets. Pull the glove away from the bottle, and the items will float slowly to the bottom. Try it again . . .and again . . .and again. This activity is mesmerizing for all preschoolers, but especially interesting to children who have autistic tendencies. It is also quite relaxing for children who are anxious or under stress. You can also place metal items in an empty bottle without oil. The glove with magnets will still attract the items; the items just don't float when they are released from the Magnetic Fingertips.

Place metal shavings in an empty bottle. They make wonderful designs as they attach to the magnets. You can get these shavings from businesses that saw metal, such as machine shops or steel fabricators. If you ask, they can empty the compartment in the saw that collects the shavings.

Materials

Plastic 20-ounce soft-drink bottle, emptied and dried out
Acetone (fingernail-polish remover)
Cloth rag
Baby oil—enough to fill the bottle almost full
Metal items—paper clips, pipe cleaners, tacks, push pins, safety pins, bingo chips with metal rim, etc.
Superglue
Electrician's tape
Children's garden glove or one-size-fits-all knit glove
5 strong magnets (purchased at craft stores)

Directions

1. Remove all labels and clean the label glue off the soft-drink bottle with acetone and a rag. The glue comes off much more easily if you remove all the paper. Make sure the bottle is cleaned out and dry; any water left in it will rust the metal pieces.

2. Drop several metal items into the bottle.

3. Now fill the bottle with baby oil.

4. Drip superglue around the inside of the cap and tightly screw it on the bottle.

5. Wrap electrician's tape around the cap of the bottle for extra reinforcement.

6. Glue strong circular magnets on each of the glove's fingertips with superglue. (Before you glue the magnets on the glove, test one magnet by rubbing it along the side of the bottle to make sure it will attract the metal pieces. If the magnet does not attract the pieces, you will need stronger magnets.)

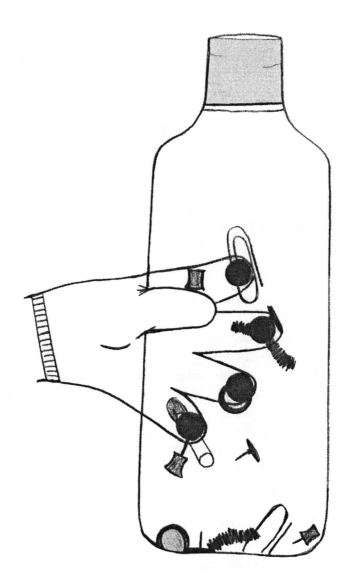

Hands-On Necklace

Transition Strategy

Have you ever worn a necklace to work and found that the toddlers were fascinated with it? They pick it up, lay it back down, and hug you hoping that it will magically transfer to their bodies. Then they look down only to find that it still is around your neck. This process is repeated over and over. With this in mind, create a Hands-On Necklace. String colorful beads, buttons, plastic bugs, or anything that will attract toddlers' attention on a sturdy cord or ribbon. A bottle of bubbles would be a wonderful addition to this necklace. Place it around your neck and "drop and flop" with a toddler, allowing him to explore each object. Have a pleasant conversation with the toddler about the colorful necklace. This is a great activity for a quiet time such as when toddlers wake up from naps or the end of the day before parents pick them up.

Variations

★ Make necklaces of different textures (smooth, bumpy, hard, soft), shapes, and colors, or with big and little objects.

★ String various key-chain fobs (choose ones that have smooth edges) on a necklace that will be safe for toddlers.

Materials

Sturdy string, cording, fish line, or ribbon
Scissors
Large needle
Various washable objects—beads
(wooden and plastic), buttons, bells, plastic bugs, rubber worms, bubbles on a rope, and so forth. Look around your room for a variety of objects. You get to use your imagination with this. Hint: The Oriental Trading catalog has many excellent items to dangle on your necklace. See appendix B for address.

Directions

1. Thread your string on a large needle. Some items may need to have a hole punched through them.

2. String objects on.

3. Tie a sturdy knot.

How Many Fingers?

Transition Strategy

While preschoolers are waiting for the bus to arrive or for the rest of the children to dress for outside, make use of your hands. Simply hold up some fingers and have the children count them and tell you how many they see. Then have them copy you with their own hands. After you've initiated this activity and children are familiar with the procedure, let them take turns being the leader. This is an excellent opportunity to keep those otherwise idle little hands busy. Conclude the activity by singing this little tune:

> "Ten Little Fingers" (tune: "Picking Up Paw-Paws")
> One little, two little, three little fingers.
> Four little, five little, six little fingers.
> Seven little, eight little, nine little fingers.
> Ten little fingers on my hands.

Variations

★ **Extender:** To determine the number of fingers everyone will hold up, roll a looped Velcro fabric cube (see appendix F) with numerals attached to it. Children can take turns rolling the cube.

★ **Extender:** Count fingers in different languages, including American Sign Language. See appendix G for ways to count in various languages.

★ **Excuser:** Once the bus arrives or the children are all dressed, excuse the preschoolers according to age by holding up that number of fingers.

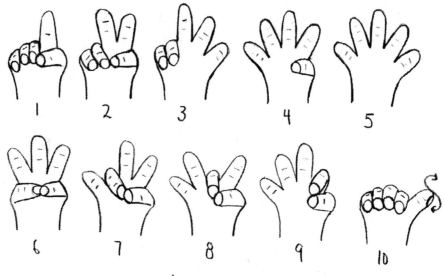

Counting in Sign Language

Counting Hands

Toddler

Transition Strategy

Counting Hands is a fun game to play with a group of children as they wait for their turn to use the bathroom or while the rest of the children finish lunch. Have children sit in a circle and put both hands out in front of them. They chant the following verse while one child walks around the circle, pointing to a different participant's hand for each word or syllable chanted:

Ibbity bibbity bown, everyone put their hands down.
Ibbity bibbity bount, round we go for the count.
Ibbity bibbity bo, how high shall we go?

The child whose hand is being pointed to when the chant ends chooses a number to count to. The pointer continues around the circle pointing to hands as the group counts to that number. Next, the last child counted chooses a hand action to do the number of times that were counted. After doing the hand action, begin the chant again. The child to the left of the one who chose the hand action is the new pointer. Continue until the waiting time is over or until children lose interest.

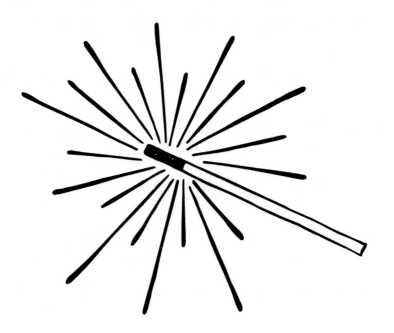

Let's Wave Good-Bye

Toddler

Transition Strategy

It is very important to greet children warmly and acknowledge them by name, both when they arrive at the center and when they arrive at other points in the day, such as group time. Greeting makes them feel welcome and secure. It is equally important for children to leave on a happy note, which makes them eager to return the next day or for another group time. This simple song does the trick.

> "Let's Wave Good-Bye" (tune: "London Bridge")
> Let's wave good-bye to (first and last name),
> (first and last name), (first and last name).
> Let's wave good-bye to (first and last name),
> We're glad you came.

Encourage the rest of the children to wave to their friends as they leave. This is an excellent song if you want to separate children as they leave group time to find their place at the lunch table or their cot for rest.

Variation

★ **Settler:** Simply changing "good-bye" in the song to "hello" allows you to use this song as a greeter to welcome and settle the children.

All-Dressed-Up Puppet

Transition Strategy

Toddlers like familiarity. They feel comfortable and secure when they see something that they recognize. Having a familiar puppet such as Baby Bear announce the next routine or activity is motivating to toddlers. If it is lunchtime, put a bib on your hand puppet and walk around the room. Show them the bib on Baby Bear by manipulating its hands to touch the bib. Talk with them about how he is getting hungry. Assure the toddlers that you realize they are getting hungry too, and encourage them to come and get their bibs on. This puppet can also indicate when it is time for other daily routines. Simply add props to the puppet: a hat for outdoor play, a security blanket for naptime, a favorite book for story time.

Preschoolers enjoy puppets too. Puppets are especially helpful to children with disabilities. Often they respond better to a puppet than to the teacher. Puppets are magically motivating and non threatening to children. If you have a child who has difficulty making it to the next activity in a timely fashion, try having the puppet excuse the children and prompt them to go directly to the next activity by waving good-bye and reassuring them that she knows they can get there quickly.
Reinforce their appropriate behavior.

Variations

* **Routine Change:** Have the puppet invite a toddler over to the diapering table or announce clean-up time to the preschoolers.

* **Attention Grabber:** Cover the All-Dressed-Up Puppet with a blanket or a piece of fabric. Move the puppet underneath the fabric as you give clues.

* **Magical Moment:** Have the puppet accompany you and the children on the move, down the hall or out to the bus. The puppet can give directions, sing a song, or do finger plays while the children are waiting.

Materials

Hand puppet with movable arms
Wire hanger
Wire cutters
Pliers
Props such as bib, diaper, hat, jacket, blanket, book, or musical instrument

Directions

1. Use any puppet with arms and hands.

2. To make a device for manipulating the puppet's hands, cut the hanger at the base of its hook and also approximately at ⅔ of the length of the bottom.

3. Use the pliers to bend a loop at each end of the hanger. The loops should fit around the puppet's "wrists."

4. Pull the puppet's hands through the loops.

5. Stretch the hanger open so that it is approximately the width of the puppet's body. Now you are ready to manipulate the puppet's hands to hold items or do hand actions.

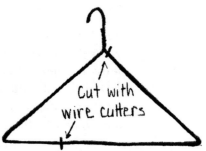

Cut with wire cutters

Bend hanger ends into loops to insert puppet hands

EXCUSER

Let Me Hand It to You

Transition Strategy

Some children have difficulty getting to their next destination without careful guidance. They may get sidetracked as they pass the block shelf or end up in the dramatic play area instead of at their cubby. But if they have something in their hands and a reason to go to the next destination, they are more apt to get there quickly. Before you excuse children, tell them where they should go and what they should do once they get there. Then hand them a ticket or a sticker that will be their pass to the next routine or activity. If possible, have one teacher positioned at the next destination to reinforce them as they turn in their ticket or attach their sticker to a designated hand-shaped board.

Variations

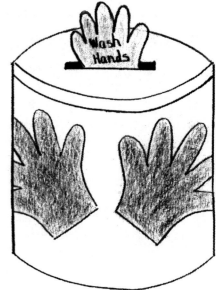

* **Routine Change:** Use the "Let Me Hand It to You" activity as preschoolers clean up the room. After they are finished, hand them a ticket or sticker to be turned in near the bathroom, at the lunch table, or at the beginning of group time.

* **Settler:** Take attendance with the tickets, giving individual recognition as preschoolers settle in for group time.

Materials

Tickets of various colors
Clear Con-Tact paper
Container
Construction paper
Water-base markers
Hand stencil
Rubber cement
Stickers
Poster board
Scissors

Directions

Tickets

1.   Trace child-size or smaller hand shapes on various colored file folders or poster board.

2.   Cover with clear Con-Tact paper.

3.   Cut out shapes.

Container

1.   Acquire a container with lid that is large enough to fit the hand shapes, such as a coffee can or frosting container.

2.   Cut a slit in the lid.

3.   Cut a piece of construction paper to fit around the container.

4.   Trace hand stencils on the construction paper and color with water-base markers.

5.   Spread rubber cement on the back of the piece of construction paper and the outside of the container, and let them dry completely.

6.   Cover the container with the construction paper.

7.   Cover the papered container with clear Con-Tact paper.

8.   Place lid on container.

Sticker Board

1.   Draw a large hand on a piece of poster board, approximately 12 by 12 inches.

2.   Cut out the hand shape.

3.   Cover with clear Con-Tact paper.

4.   Cut off excess Con-Tact paper.

5.   Attach to wall near the destination to which you will send the children. Children will enjoy looking at this board with many colorful stickers as they wait.

3

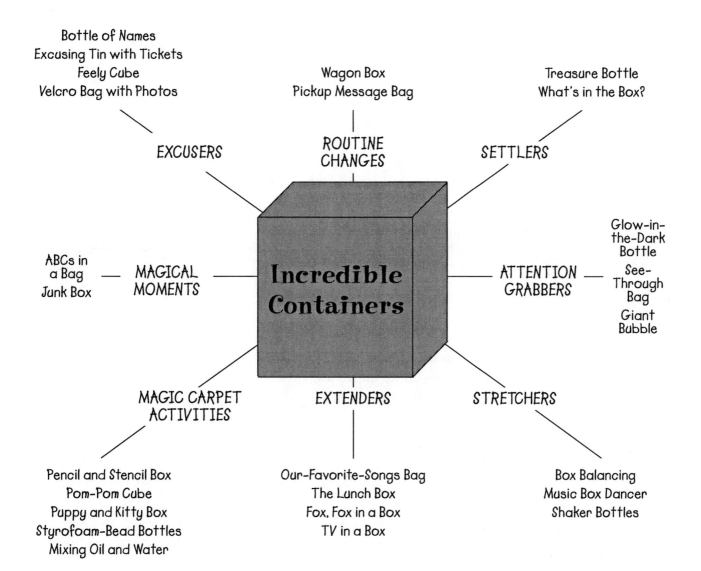

Bottle of Names
Excusing Tin with Tickets
Feely Cube
Velcro Bag with Photos

EXCUSERS

Wagon Box
Pickup Message Bag

ROUTINE
CHANGES

Treasure Bottle
What's in the Box?

SETTLERS

Glow-in-
the-Dark
Bottle

ABCs in
a Bag
Junk Box

MAGICAL
MOMENTS

Incredible
Containers

ATTENTION
GRABBERS

See-
Through
Bag

Giant
Bubble

MAGIC CARPET
ACTIVITIES

EXTENDERS

STRETCHERS

Pencil and Stencil Box
Pom-Pom Cube
Puppy and Kitty Box
Styrofoam-Bead Bottles
Mixing Oil and Water

Our-Favorite-Songs Bag
The Lunch Box
Fox, Fox in a Box
TV in a Box

Box Balancing
Music Box Dancer
Shaker Bottles

Wagon Box

Transition Strategy

Toddlers love to push and pull things. Why not try a Wagon Box for clean-up time? This simply made wagon is perfect for toddlers who like to slide along the floor. They will have great fun picking up the toys, putting them in the box, and then pushing or pulling the box over to the shelf where they unload them. This activity is developmentally appropriate for toddlers and makes clean-up time enjoyable.

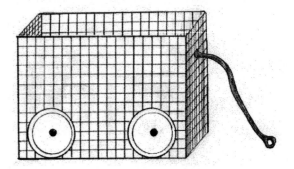

Variation

* Toddlers enjoy sitting in the box. Put a couple of board books in for them to look at during a waiting time.

Materials

1 medium-size box
Heavy cording, 30 inches
Colorful Con-Tact paper (enough to cover the box inside and outside)
4 plastic margarine tub covers
4 large brass fasteners
Duct tape

Directions

1. Fold top flaps inside the box to reinforce it, or if using a box with a lid, set the box inside the lid for reinforcement.

2. Attach the margarine-tub covers at each corner with brass fasteners. (For safety, cover the fastener on the inside with duct tape). Make sure the "wheels" are even with the bottom edge of the box, so they don't snap off.

3. Cover inside and outside of box, including bottom, with Con-Tact paper.

4. Make a hole in the middle of one box end and attach the cord. Knot both ends of the cord, one inside the box and the other at the pulling end of the cord.

ROUTINE
CHANGE

Pickup Message Bag

Transition Strategy

Are you looking for a novel way to get children to clean up after the last activity? Try using a Pickup Message Bag. In a fabric or paper gift bag, put a variety of pickup messages such as "After you pick up the paper scraps, go wash your hands," "(name of child), please pick up four blocks," or "(name of child), put all the scissors away." When it's time to begin cleaning up, pull a message out of the bag to read to each child. Children will respond to these directions because it is not your usual way of instructing them at clean-up time.

Variation

★ **Routine Change:** Write clean-up directions that the children give you. They are more invested in clean-up because they have offered ideas for the message bag.

Directions

1. Glue picture of children cleaning up on outside of paper gift bag (optional).

2. To gather message ideas, observe clean-up time and record pickup statements that are made by you or other staff.

3. Write messages on slips of paper—as many messages as there are children in your group.

4. Place messages in bag.

Treasure Bottle

Transition Strategy

As children are finding their individual seating spaces for circle time, help them settle by finding out what is in your Treasure Bottle. This bottle contains items that children treasure—little toys, jewelry, rocks—things you've discovered they love by tuning in to their interests. As each child is seated, give him a clue about an item in your bottle he would particularly like. Continue with the clues until the object is guessed. You may need to caution children that "this is Jamie's turn, so let him guess right now." When the child guesses correctly, take out the item with a long pair of tweezers. Continue this process with each child. Make sure there are enough items in the jar so all will have an opportunity to guess. Simplify or complicate your clues depending on the developmental abilities of the children.

Variations

*   **Settler:** Finding a message in a bottle is always exciting. Use a plastic bottle and write a message to announce a special event for the day or write the day's schedule. Create a little drama about finding this bottle with a message in it for your class. As children come to group, pull out a message and read it to them. It's another way to emphasize the importance of reading.

*   **Settler:** Messages in the bottle can also be love notes, or fond words that describe the children. As children settle into group, they can draw out a slip of paper. Use concrete phrases such as "You're curious," "You're generous," or "You are friendly."

Materials

Clean plastic mayonnaise or peanut-butter jar with an opening that will accommodate small items
Items children love and are familiar with, such as little action figures, manipulatives, rings, polished rocks, keys, or trinkets
Con-Tact paper
Optional: Long tweezers (if the opening is too small for your hand)

Directions

1. Cover the plastic jar or bottle with Con-Tact paper.

2. Place items in the jar.

SETTLER

What's in the Box?

Transition Strategy

Children will settle into group time more easily if one adult is waiting for them, prepared with something from your "bag of tricks." Children love wrapped packages, so use a box wrapped with gift paper and topped with a bow. Choose an object to put inside the box that would be of interest to the children, such as a new toy you're introducing, a picture of the children, or something from the art activity that they will do next. Give the package to the first child coming to the group area. Let her shake it and guess what might be inside. As each child joins the group, the package is passed on. Each child has an opportunity to guess what might be inside. You can prompt critical thinking by asking questions such as "What would make a sound like that?" or "Is it heavy or light?" When all children are at group, you can open the package and reveal the contents that might lead to your next activity. Children will eagerly come to group time each day knowing something new will be in the wrapped box.

Variations

* **Settler:** When you wrap the box, wrap it in multiple layers of gift wrap or tissue. Instead of focusing just on the object inside, you can explain that this is a special package because it has many layers of wrapping. Each child gets to carefully unwrap one layer of paper before passing it on to the next child. As children are unwrapping, you can say, "Do you think this is the last layer?" "What color do you think the next paper is?" or "What do you think is inside?" Children's fascination with unwrapping will settle them for the next activity. Note: This is not appropriate for large groups where children must wait for a long time.

* **Extender:** Place a letter of the alphabet on each of the six sides of the box. Have children pass the box, each taking a turn identifying one of the letters. Older preschoolers can identify a letter that is the first letter of their name. Or children can identify objects in the room that start with the same sound as one of the letters, such as B for ball, blocks, and so on.

Materials

Gift box with a lid
Gift wrap or colored tissue paper
Bow
Tape

Directions

1. Gift wrap the box and the lid separately, so the lid can be removed from the box without unwrapping it.

2. Add a fancy bow.

Glow-in-the-Dark Bottle

Transition Strategy

Children are naturally curious, so when you turn off the light for this attention grabber, you'll certainly have their attention. Before turning off the light, settle the children. Then show them the special Glow-in-the-Dark Bottle you have to share with them today. Create a little suspense by telling the children you need to turn off the light so they can see what you have in your special bottle. Once it is dark, bring out the bottle again—the dark objects suspended in the mineral oil will glow. Shake the bottle and watch the objects float to the bottom. The suspense holds the children's attention until you're ready to move to the next activity.

Variations

* **Settler:** Children can use these bottles during rest time as a soothing activity.
* **Magic Carpet Activity:** Set out during Magic Carpet activity time, when children have a few minutes prior to the next activity.

Materials

10- or 20-ounce plastic soda bottle and cap
Mineral oil or baby oil
Glow-in-the-dark objects, such as erasers or 1-inch porcupine balls
    (Oriental Trading catalog—see appendix B)
Superglue
Duct tape

Directions

1.   Drop a variety of glow-in-the-dark objects into the bottle.

2.   Fill the bottle with oil, about ⅔ full.

3.   Superglue the cap onto the bottle.

4.   Wrap the cap with duct tape so the bottle doesn't leak.

See-Through Bag

Transition Strategy

A fun way to get children's attention is to bring in a mesh bag with a couple of fun items children are familiar with, such as a beanbag toy, a movie action figure, or something that is related to your current topic. Say to the children, "I brought my bag today; do you think you can guess what's inside my bag?" Of course they can see it! They get all excited when they tell you what it is. You can say, "Well, how did you know!" Continue acting surprised as children tell you the bag has holes in it. They will think it's wonderful fun if you pretend that you can't understand how they can guess.

Variation

* **Magical Moment:** Take a smaller version of the mesh bag with you when you're on the move, going down the hall or out to the bus. It can serve a second purpose of carrying other transitional items with you to keep children engaged while they're waiting.

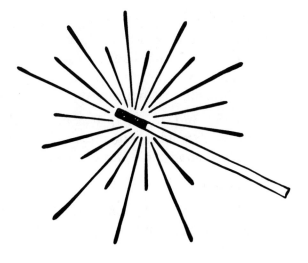

Giant Bubble

Transition Strategy

Do you want an inviting place for group time? Would you like an area that motivates children to come to group? Consider having your group time in a giant air-filled bubble—a 9-by-12-foot bubble you create with heavy plastic sheeting and a small fan. Children will be motivated to wash up or clean up quickly so they can get into the bubble. Once they are inside, the quiet atmosphere created by the bubble has a calming effect on the children. A small group of children and one teacher will fit quite comfortably in the bubble. Bring in children's sit-upons, or stick circles cut from Con-Tact adhesive paper to the floor of the bubble. Group time activities can include stories, singing, felt-board activities, and quiet circle games. Before children go into the bubble, establish and emphasize the safety rules: quiet play; sock feet; staying away from the tunnel and fan. Post these rules by the door as a reminder. Once inside, position yourself in front of the fan tunnel as an added precaution. You might want to place a small stop sign at the inside entrance of the tunnel.

Caution: Some children will initially be afraid to go into the bubble. Do not force them. Usually they will see that it is fun and will enter after a while. Play in the plastic bubble should always be teacher supervised.

Variations

★ **Settler:** Another settler activity is to have the children decorate the walls with colored Con-Tact adhesive paper shapes. Add items such as flowers, sun, trees, grass, birds and bees, and a pond to the scene each day. This could be a fun way to begin your group time.

★ Be creative and cut your plastic into another shape reflecting a teaching theme, such as a heart or a turtle. Try black plastic instead of clear to teach about the moon and stars or other science activities.

Materials

6-mil clear plastic sheeting (the type you lay when painting or use to cover outside windows), 12 by 18 feet
Iron
Cotton dish towel or old pillow case
Duct tape
2-inch-wide clear plastic mailing tape
20-inch square window fan
Electrical outlet

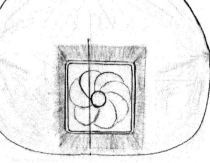

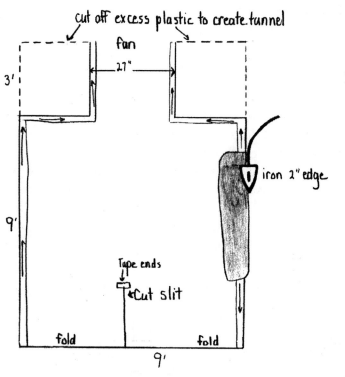

Directions

1. Fold the plastic in half. Now you have a double thickness of plastic about 12 by 9 feet.

2. On the side opposite the fold, create the tunnel by measuring and cutting 40 inches in from each side, and 3 feet from the back edge. Now you have a 9-by-9-foot bubble with a 3-foot tunnel in the middle of the back. A bubble this size will seat about six children comfortably, but you can make your bubble larger or smaller depending on the purpose you will use it for. Always leave at least a 3-foot tunnel so the children are not too close to the fan that will be at the end of this tunnel.

3. Fold your cotton dish towel over the raw edge of the plastic so you have material under and on top with the two layers of plastic in between. This will protect the plastic from the warm iron. With your iron set on medium heat, iron the area that is covered by the cotton fabric about 2 inches into the plastic. The two layers of plastic will melt together, closing off the edges. Move your cotton fabric along the raw edges of the plastic (sides and back of the bubble and sides of tunnel), ironing as you go. Remember to leave an opening at the end of the tunnel for your fan.

4. Cut about a 2-foot slit in the middle of the front of the bubble (opposite the tunnel—see illustration) for the entrance (on the fold this will be a 4-foot opening). To secure the ends of your slit so it doesn't tear, put a 2-inch strip of clear tape on both the inside and outside of each end of the slit.

5. Fit the box fan into the tunnel and secure with duct tape all around the fan.

6. Turn the fan on high to blow the large plastic bubble up with air. Once it's filled, turn your fan to medium and keep the fan running while the bubble is in use.

7. Before turning off the fan, make sure all children are out of the bubble. Then turn off the fan and let the bubble deflate. The bubble folds up quite small when not in use, so it doesn't require a lot of storage space.

STRETCHER

Box Balancing

Transition Strategy

Toddlers love this little balancing game—they will do it over and over. Start with a small box and ask a child to put it on top of his head, balancing it there until you count to three. The child will let it fall when you reach "three," and want to do it all over. Ask children to balance the box on other parts of their bodies, such as a foot, an elbow, or a hand. This strategy helps build eye-hand coordination as children bend to pick up the box and balance it on a body part. For a greater challenge for preschoolers, ask them to balance two boxes at the same time.

Variations

* **Attention Grabber:** Put something tiny in a little box. As the children sit down for group time move to them and give each a quick peek. Tell them to keep it a secret until everyone has seen.

* **Extender:** Hide little boxes around the room. Send pairs of children out with an assignment to find a red box, a blue box, or a yellow box.

* **Magical Moment:** It's easy to take a little box with you when you're on the move. Play a "shell game" by hiding a box under one of three of the children's hats. This game challenges children's visual memory and keeps them engaged while they are waiting.

STRETCHER # Music Box Dancer

Transition Strategy

Music boxes motivate children to get up and move. Anticipate when children will need to get up, stretch, and move during an activity, and use a wind-up music box with a dancer on top to get them moving. Bring out a music box and show them how the ballerina twirls around. Wind up the music box, and as it plays, ask the children to get up and twirl around like a ballerina. See if they can dance on their tiptoes. Ask a parent to sew some simple tutus that you can use during the Music Box Dancer transition or in a special learning center. When the Music Box Dancer winds down, the children can too. After the break, they will be able to attend better to the next group activity.

Variations

* **Routine Change:** Use a different music box (that plays a different song) to signal a new activity.

* **Magical Moment:** Take miniature music boxes with you when you take the children down the hall for lunch or to the toilet.

* **Excuser:** Purchase several push-button music boxes. Excuse children by saying, "When Allyson, Antonio, and Kirk hear 'Twinkle, Twinkle,' they can get their jackets on." When that music box stops, choose three more children and play another song.

Shaker Bottles

Transition Strategy

Anticipate when children need to get up and move around. For such times, have Shaker Bottles ready for each child to use while listening to music. The shakers will help them focus on marching or moving to the music. If you fill them with different materials, each Shaker Bottle will make a different sound. This is an excellent transitional activity for children who have attention deficits and who need to do stretchers frequently.

Materials

Empty plastic bottles (water or soft-drink or baby bottles; small juice bottles are the perfect size for toddlers)
"Fill" items such as colored noodles or rice (directions follow), beans, popcorn, jelly beans
Superglue
Duct tape
Tape player and musical tapes
Optional: colored tape or stickers

For colored noodles or rice:
1 bottle of rubbing alcohol
Liquid food coloring
Large bowl or plastic bag
Rice, or noodles such as elbows or bowties

Directions

1.   Pour ½–1 inch of filler material into bottle.

2.   Glue around the jar's mouth, then screw on the cap.

3.   Decorate the outside of the bottle with colored tape or stickers.

Colored Noodles or Rice

1.   Pour one 12-ounce bottle of rubbing alcohol into a bowl. Stir in approximately 10 drops (more if you want more vibrant colors) of food coloring and mix in 1–2 cups uncooked noodles or rice into bowl. Or, put the alcohol, food coloring, and noodles or rice in a large self-closing plastic bag and mix.

2.   After a few minutes, remove the noodles or rice with a slotted spoon, or drain through a sieve, and lay on paper towel to dry.

3.   If you started with a primary color (red, yellow, or blue), you can now add another primary color to the same rubbing alcohol to get a secondary color. For example, add yellow to blue to get green.

EXTENDER

Our-Favorite-Songs Bag

Transition Strategy

If group time is winding down and you find you have a few minutes to fill, pull out your Our-Favorite-Songs Bag. Children will be excited to draw a song card from the bag, choosing a song for the group to sing. In fact, it might be a card that they helped make! Children love singing their old favorites, even if it isn't the "right" season of the year. This activity gives children an opportunity to develop prereading skills and is wonderful for toddlers who thrive on repetition and love taking things out of (and putting them back into) bags.

Variation

* **Magical Moment:** Take the Our-Favorite-Songs Bag with you for those Magical Moments you need to fill on a field trip, waiting for the bus, or waiting during bathroom break.

Materials

Fabric bag
Fabric paint
2-by-3-inch cards
Stickers or pictures that represent favorite songs
Marker

Directions

1. Find a cheerful, colorful bag and use fabric paint to print on the side, "Our Favorite Songs."

2. Print children's favorite songs, one title per card. Add appropriate pictures to each card as added cues. Have the children help you make these little cards, and they will become more meaningful.

The Lunch Box

Transition Strategy

If it's lunchtime and lunch has not arrived, fill those minutes by playing "The Lunch Box," a game that will challenge children's visual memory! Tell the children you have something new in your lunch box. Open the box and take out the items inside, one by one, laying them on the floor so all can see. Use items that might be in a child's lunchbox, such as a plastic fork and spoon, a plate or bowl, a small tablecloth, a napkin, salt and pepper shakers, a Thermos, or a box of raisins or nuts. Discuss the items and ask the children to tell you about them. After children have looked at the items, put them all back in the box and close the lid. Then ask the children to tell you, from memory, what's in the box. As each item is correctly identified, take it out and place it on the floor. You may have to give hints for the last items. Change the items in The Lunch Box from time to time to refresh children's interest in this activity.

Fox, Fox in a Box

Transition Strategy

Nothing engages children more than hide-and-seek games. Use a set of nested boxes and a small stuffed fox to extend your group time when you have a few extra minutes. Set out in a row the largest boxes in your set of nested boxes. Ask the children to cover their eyes while you put a stuffed fox in one of the boxes and cover it with the lid. Ask children to open their eyes while you shuffle the boxes around. Chant with the children, "Fox, Fox in the box. Fox, Fox in the box." Then choose one child to pick a color and chant together, "Fox, Fox, are you in the <u>red</u> box?" Open the red box and see if it's a correct guess. Continue guessing until the correct box is chosen. Children of all ages, including toddlers, love this game and will want you to hide the fox again and again!

Variations

* **Settler:** Use the nesting boxes without the stuffed fox as a settler. At group time, have your set of nested boxes ready. As each child joins the group, she removes the outside or largest box and sets the box out so all can see. The next box is stacked on the first one, and so on. While this activity is taking place, sing with children to the tune of "Skip to My Lou": "What oh what might be in the next box? What oh what might be in the next box?

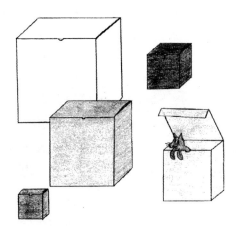

What oh what might be in the next box? Guess now if you can." In the last box, have a message indicating what they will talk about or do next.

* **Attention Grabber:** Use the Fox, Fox in a Box game as an attention grabber.

Materials

Sets of 5–8 nested boxes, or cube-shaped boxes of graduated sizes (so that one fits into another) with lids
A variety of colored Con-Tact papers (if making your own nested boxes)
Small stuffed fox
Optional: object or message

Directions

If making your own nested boxes, cover each box and its lid with a different color of Con-Tact paper.

EXTENDER

TV in a Box

Transition Strategy

Introduce this "TV" box when you have a few minutes at the end of group time. The children will be able to watch one of their favorite nursery rhymes on "TV"—one that you created. As children are excused one at a time to wash their hands, you can continue to scroll the nursery rhymes on the screen as children say them with you.

Variations

* Put children "on TV" by enlarging their photos on a color copier. Tape them together to form your roll. Imagine how toddlers will feel when they see themselves "on TV"!

* **Attention Grabber:** Make rolls that focus on different topics, and change them from time to time. Make a roll that introduces a new concept or topic such as safety rules. Use it as an attention grabber at the beginning of group.

* **Magic Carpet Activity:** Leave the "TV" out during Magic Carpet time for children to watch, read, or sing along while they wait. Children can easily manipulate the scrolls for themselves.

Materials

Cardboard box (a small copy paper box or cereal box would work well)
Con-Tact paper
Scissors
A roll of shelving paper or craft paper cut to the width of box and to the
    length necessary for the story or the number of nursery rhymes you've
    chosen
Nursery-rhyme pictures from a coloring book
Two 1-inch diameter dowels, approximately 6 inches longer than the width
    of your box
Masking tape
Markers
Optional: photos of your children enlarged on a photocopier

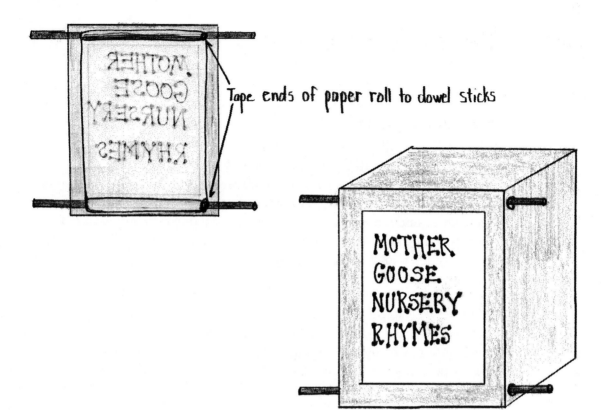

Tape ends of paper roll to dowel sticks

MOTHER
GOOSE
NURSERY
RHYMES

Directions

1. Remove cover or open box flaps.

2. Cut a large square in one face of the box. This will be the "TV screen."

3. Make two holes in each "side" panel, top and bottom, for the dowels. Insert a dowel through the top two holes and another through the bottom two holes. See illustration.

4. Prepare the picture roll by tracing or drawing the nursery-rhyme pictures on the roll of paper, going from top to bottom. Use one picture for each nursery rhyme. Pictures should be the size that fills up the square you cut in your box. Leave a blank "leader" space at the beginning.

5. Color the pictures and add the name of the nursery rhyme.

6. Attach the bottom of the picture roll, pictures facing out, to the bottom dowel with masking tape. Roll the paper onto the bottom dowel by turning it.

7. Attach the top of the picture roll to the other dowel.

8. Now roll paper onto the top dowel to position the first picture in the screen.

9. Spread Con-Tact paper on the box and the cover or flaps, allowing for the cover or flaps to be opened easily so you can change rolls.

Pencil and Stencil Box

Transition Strategy

Fill a small box with plain paper, colored pencils, unusual rulers, and stencils for shapes that interest your children. Keep the box on your Magic Carpet shelf and allow preschoolers to explore the materials and use them for printing their names or for drawing. Some children may ignore the rulers and stencils and do their own creating. Others will enjoy tracing the stencils and making lines with the rulers. This is a good emerging-literacy activity, quick to pick up and easy to clean up by returning all the supplies back to the box.

Variations

* Fill a box with paper, rubber stamps, and washable stamp pads. Preschoolers also enjoy stamping markers. There are even rubber-stamp sets for the alphabet in sign language, including signs for phrases such as "I love you."

* Paper and markers are another simple but enjoyable Magic Carpet activity. Markers leave bright colors and are easy to manipulate for the child who has poor muscle control, because they are larger in diameter and easier to grasp than pencils.

* Children love putting stickers on paper! Collect sticker odds and ends and place them in a small tin or box. Let children spend time picking out stickers and using their small-muscle skills to decorate the paper included in the Pencil and Stencil Box.

Materials

Box about the size of a pencil box, a shoe box, or a large pencil pouch—
    decorate and label it so children know the contents
Plain paper the size of the box or pouch
Rulers—straight and curved
Stencils—the plastic ones with various shapes, letters, and numerals
    work well
A small table where a couple of children can work cooperatively, or
    lap desks

MAGIC
CARPET
ACTIVITY

Pom-Pom Cube

Transition Strategy

This cardboard cube is guaranteed to engage toddlers in an activity they love. Several toddlers at one time can put the pom-poms through one of the many holes in the cube. When they've put them all in, they will want to take them all out and start over. Because the cube is sturdy, you will find it perfect for sitting on—which toddlers will want to do!

Variation

★ Instead of using yarn pom-poms with the cube, use small purchased sponge shapes or beanbags. Each item has its own texture, which is excellent for children who need to experience a variety of sensory stimuli.

Materials

6 heavy cardboard squares (12 by 12 inches) with 5 holes each (check with your local printing shop for these); or make these 5-hole boards using a jigsaw

Brightly colored Con-Tact paper

Colored duct tape

30 4-inch yarn pom-poms (directions for making the pom-poms are found in appendix F, or pom-poms can be purchased at craft stores)

Directions

1. Cover each cardboard square with Con-Tact paper. Cut the Con-Tact paper around the edge of each hole.

2. Begin assembling the cube by attaching the first two squares together with duct tape. Continue to assemble with the duct tape until you've completed a cube. Reinforce the edges with duct tape on the outside and the inside. This makes a pretty sturdy box with holes.

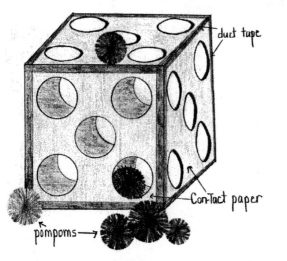

Puppy and Kitty Box

Transition Strategy

In a Puppy and Kitty Box, children will find small stuffed puppies and kitties and a small cardboard cube that has a kitty or puppy sticker and a number on each side of the cube. Playing with a partner, children roll this cube or "die" and count out the correct number of that animal. This is a wonderful opportunity for a child with a disability to pair up with another child who can model the game. While this allows preschoolers to practice taking turns, activity boxes like this also lend themselves to individual play—toddlers will take the pieces out, line them up, and simply play with them.

Variation

★ **Extender:** Give each child one of the stuffed animals from the activity box. Roll the cube. If the number two comes up, ask two children to put their animals in the box. Continue until all are back in the box.

Materials

Small plastic box (such as lunch or school box or tin)—look for a container that is decorated with the theme you're using, such as kitties and puppies, or add stickers to match the theme

Small stuffed or plastic toys, such as kitties, puppies, dinosaurs, sea creatures

Small cardboard cube

Theme-related stickers to put on the cube

Marker

Directions

1. Decide the activity box theme.

2. Using a cube stencil in a stencil-cutting machine, make a small cube (1¼ inch).

3. Place one sticker on each side of the cube. Use three kitties and three puppies.

4. With the marker, write a number on each side of the cube. Use numbers that your children will be able to count. Some children will need smaller numbers, in which case you could use numbers from 1 to 3 and repeat them.

5. Place the stuffed or plastic animals and the assembled cube in the box.

6. Decorate the outside of the box with stickers to identify the theme.

Styrofoam-Bead Bottles

Special Needs

Transition Strategy

Most of us find water very soothing. Styrofoam-Bead Bottles are appropriate for all children but will be particularly soothing for children with attention deficit, autism, or sensory deficits. When a child needs to be calmed or soothed, give her a bottle to hold. She will rotate it to watch the beads and glitter shift from one bottle to the other. By putting it against her ear, she can hear the soothing sound it makes. For children who have a difficult time settling down at nap time, this quiet, soothing bottle has a very calming effect.

Styrofoam beads

tornado tube

colored water

glitter

Materials

2 plastic 16-ounce soft-drink bottles
Tiny Styrofoam beads (used in large beanbag
    chairs or purchased at some fabric stores)
A tornado tube (purchased from school supply
    catalogs or stores)
Colorful plastic glitter
Water
Food coloring
Duct tape

Directions

1. Chip or drill out the plastic ridge in the center of the tornado tube without damaging the threads. You want the full diameter of the tube.

2. Attach the tube to one of the two bottles.

3. Put glitter into the bottle and fill with water up to the top of the tube.

4. Add a few drops of food coloring (your choice).

5. Fill the second bottle with Styrofoam beads, about ¾ full. (The smaller beads work best.) Add ½ cup water to that bottle.

6. Over a sink, put the second bottle in the other end of the tornado tube and screw together.

7. Cover the tornado tube and the neck of each bottle with duct tape if you are concerned about leakage.

Mixing Oil and Water

Special Needs

Toddler

Transition Strategy

Mixing oil and water allows your children to observe science at work! Assemble several bottles that contain oil and water, creating variety by adding color to some of the bottles. Make these available for children who complete a group activity early and have a few minutes before the next activity. Children love to manipulate these oil and water bottles and watch what happens to the layers of oil and water. When they shake the bottles, the contents will look sparkly until the water and oil separate out again. The two-color oil and water bottles will make a new color when shaken. The bubbles in this combination are larger and mix more slowly. Vary the contents for different effects.

Materials

Plastic 20-ounce soft-drink bottles, or smaller plastic juice bottles for toddlers
Mineral oil
Baby oil
Corn syrup
Food coloring (primary colors)
Wax colorant chips (primary colors—available in candle-making sections of craft stores)
Water
Superglue
Duct tape
Plastic confetti in various shapes

Directions

Bottle One

1. Fill half the bottle with equal parts mineral oil and baby oil. (Baby oil has a different consistency from mineral oil.)

2. Color water with food coloring and add to oil. The bottle should be full to the bottom of the bottle neck.

3. Put glue inside cap, screw onto bottle, and reinforce with duct tape.

Bottle Two

1. Fill a baby juice bottle half full with mineral or baby oil.

2. Add a ¼-inch chip of wax colorant of a primary color to the oil.

3. Color enough water with food coloring in a different primary color, and add water to fill up the bottle.

4. Put some glue on inside of cap, tightly screw onto bottle, and reinforce with duct tape.

Bottle Three

1. Fill a 20-ounce or smaller bottle with baby oil.

2. Add colorful confetti shapes to match a current theme, such as dinosaurs, shapes, or numbers. Toddlers like these bottles because the confetti moves more slowly through the baby oil.

Bottle Four

1. A bottle of ants is another fun bottle for children. Fill a 20-ounce bottle about ¼ to ⅓ full with corn syrup.

2. Add little plastic ants or confetti. The corn syrup and the ants move very slowly. Children love to watch them as they slide down the bottle.

ABCs in a Bag

Transition Strategy

Take a bag of alphabet cards with you when you're on the move with older preschoolers (out to the bus or down the hall). Use waiting time with the children to work on letter recognition. Have children draw a card from the alphabet bag. Ask them to identify the letter, and ask them to think of words that begin with that letter. You might also ask them to find objects in their immediate surroundings that begin with the letter. All children who are waiting can participate in these activities.

Variation

Instead of an alphabet bag, make a numbers or shapes bag.

Materials

Bag, such as a gift bag or a looped Velcro fabric bag with handles
Deck of alphabet cards (purchase or make)
Optional: Fabric paint

For deck of cards:
Poster board
Adhesive letters and stickers

Directions

1. Use a fabric or paper gift bag, or make your own. If you can find an alphabet-print fabric, that's perfect. Otherwise, use fabric paint and print "ABC Bag" and some letters of the alphabet scattered around.

2. Purchase alphabet cards or make them by cutting poster board into playing-card-size cards.

3. On each card place one letter and a sticker showing something that starts with that letter.

Junk Box

Transition Strategy

Take a Junk Box with you when you're out of the classroom and know you'll have a few extra minutes with the children. Open the Junk Box and let children examine the contents. Then let them select an item from the box to talk about or use. Nature stores will provide interesting ideas for items you can throw into a Junk Box. The sky is the limit when thinking of the possibilities for a Junk Box.

Variation

★ **Extender:** This interesting Junk Box can be used for multiple transitions throughout the day. Use items from the Junk Box as an extender when you have a few extra minutes, or when children are settling into group time.

Materials

A small lunch or school box; if it has a handle, all the better for taking it with you for those Magical Moments

"Junk" items of interest to children, such as a tiny cube magnifying glass, a tiny box of books, Peek-a-Boo riddle cards (see page 110), a bottle of bubbles, a squishy stress ball, tops, a pretend microphone, colorful feathers, novel key chains, plastic animals, or a miniature kaleidoscope

Bottle of Names

Transition Strategy

Sometimes it's best if one child at a time is excused at the end of the day. A nifty way to do this is to use a Bottle of Names. A ribbon that is attached to a name card is pulled out of the bottle. It's sort of like fishing, waiting to see if your name is the next one to be "caught." This eliminates the rush and congestion of excusing all the children at one time.

Variation

★ **Settler:** Instead of children's names, write concepts or facts of interest about the topic you're teaching, such as "The name of the shape that's round like a ball is a _____." These can be read to children as a settler or for an extender at group time.

Materials

Plastic bottle with large mouth, or quart jar
5 yards of ¼-inch-wide satin ribbon (different colors)
File folder
Stapler
Marker

Directions

1. Cut 1-by-5-inch strips from file folder, one for each child.

2. Print a child's name on each strip.

3. Cut ribbon into 9-inch lengths and staple one to each name card.

4. Put the paper strips in the bottle and let the colorful ribbons hang outside the bottle.

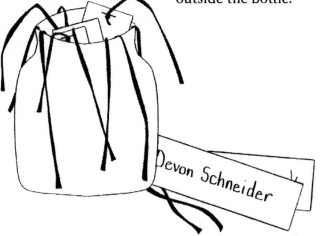

EXCUSER

Excusing Tin
with Tickets

Transition Strategy

Teachers frequently have individual children take care of a routine task, such as hand washing, during a group activity. To make this transition go smoothly, give children a "ticket" (a small card with a sticker on it), to which you have a matching "ticket." During the group activity, the teacher can hold up a ticket from her tin that signals the child with the matching sticker to quietly go and wash hands. This allows the teacher and the children to continue on with the activity with minimal disruption! As children leave, they put their "tickets" back in the tin. For children who are easily distracted, holding on to tickets will serve as a reminder of where they have to go—to wash their hands. If they are still holding their tickets, they haven't carried out the routine.

Materials

Two clean salted-nut tins with plastic covers
Printed Con-Tact paper
Foam-rubber place mats
Stickers, in pairs

Directions

1. From the place mats, cut enough "tickets" for each child in your class plus a matching set for yourself.

2. Adhere a sticker to each ticket. When you make the set, have one animal for each child. Make yourself a set, one of each sticker.

3. Cover the two tins with Con-Tact paper of two different colors, or cover with the same color and mark one to be the children's tin and the other, the teacher's tin.

4. Place each set of tickets in a tin.

Feely Cube

Transition Strategy

Use a Feely Cube to excuse children from group time. Fill the cube with sponge shapes in a variety of colors. Children will like the tactile effect as they pull out pieces. Ask a child to name the color of a piece and then excuse all the children who are wearing that color. You can also ask each child to identify the shape as it is pulled out of the Feely Cube and then direct her to the next activity. This cube is easily stored by flattening it down.

Variations

★ **Attention Grabber:** As children come to the circle, have them reach in to find an object.

★ **Extender:** Have children reach in to find an object. (Include small objects with different textures and interesting shapes.) Explain that they are to use their sense of touch to guess what is inside. Ask them to find one object and hold it inside the cube. (Their tendency is to pull the object out and look at it.) Use open-ended questions to help them guess what they are feeling.

★ **Magical Moment:** Use when toddlers are waiting their turn to have their diapers changed. Toddlers will be content to take the objects out and put them back in, and they have fun seeing what they might pull out.

Materials

A Velcro fabric cube—see directions in appendix F with the modifications given under "Directions"
Art-foam shapes or colored pieces

Directions

1. Sew the Velcro fabric cube according to the directions in appendix F, but don't fill with fiberfill.

2. Cut an X in the center of one side, large enough for a child's hand to reach through.

3. Purchase art-foam shapes of different colors or shapes (triangle, circle, square, or animal shapes).

4. Fill cube with art-foam pieces.

EXCUSER

Velcro Bag with Photos

Transition Strategy

Have your Velcro Bag with Photos ready any time you need to excuse children to go home or to the next activity. Stored inside your bag are photos of children in protective photo holders, with pieces of hooked-fabric stripping on the back. Reach inside, pull out a photo, and stick it on the outside of the bag. That child is excused, and the remaining children will eagerly await the next photo. This photo-visual works especially well for children who have trouble attending to directions.

Variations

★ **Excuser:** Put small stuffed animals in the looped-fabric bag to excuse children. Choose a child to come up and pull an animal out of the bag. That child chooses a friend, and both move to their next destination the way that animal would move. They hop like rabbits, for example, or walk on all fours like bears.

★ Fill your bag with stuffed animals to send on the bus. Each child can hold one of the animals on his ride home.

★ Have your stretcher, extender, or Magical Moment props in the bag. Keep it handy for the right transitions.

Materials

Looped Velcro fabric, 20 by 40 inches
Sewing machine
Thread
Photos of children
Plastic photo holders (4 by 6 inches), purchased at office supply stores or photography shops

Directions for photos

1. Take individual photos of children in your class.

2. Put each one in a photo holder.

3. Attach a small piece of hooked-Velcro stripping to the back of the photo holder.

Directions for the bag

1. Fold the looped Velcro fabric in half with right sides together, to make it 20 by 20 inches. Sew two of the edges, leaving the top edge open.

2. Fold down the open edge 1 inch and sew the hem.

3. Turn right side out.

4. For the handles, cut two strips of looped Velcro fabric 2 by 10 inches. Fold lengthwise and sew, with wrong sides together (seam will be on the outside but won't fray). Sew the two ends of one handle strip to one side of the bag and the two ends of the other handle strip to the other side.

4

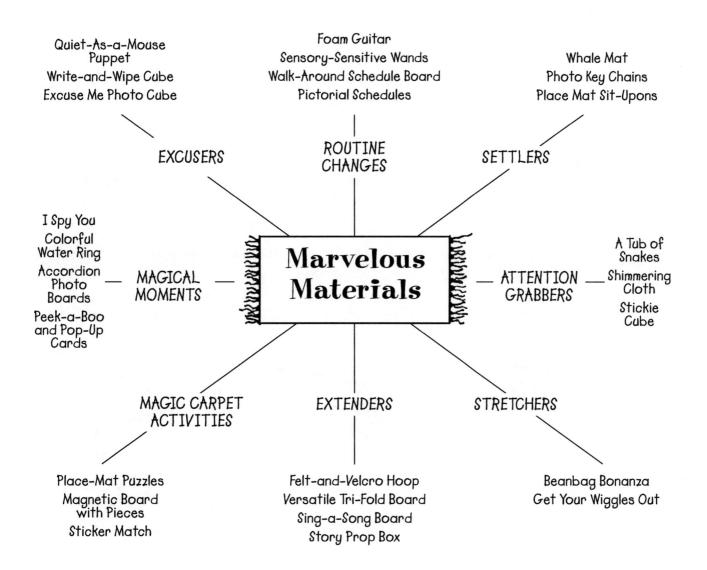

Quiet-As-a-Mouse
Puppet
Write-and-Wipe Cube
Excuse Me Photo Cube

EXCUSERS

Foam Guitar
Sensory-Sensitive Wands
Walk-Around Schedule Board
Pictorial Schedules

ROUTINE
CHANGES

Whale Mat
Photo Key Chains
Place Mat Sit-Upons

SETTLERS

I Spy You
Colorful
Water Ring
Accordion
Photo
Boards
Peek-a-Boo
and Pop-Up
Cards

MAGICAL
MOMENTS

**Marvelous
Materials**

ATTENTION
GRABBERS

A Tub of
Snakes
Shimmering
Cloth
Stickie
Cube

MAGIC CARPET
ACTIVITIES

EXTENDERS

STRETCHERS

Place-Mat Puzzles
Magnetic Board
with Pieces
Sticker Match

Felt-and-Velcro Hoop
Versatile Tri-Fold Board
Sing-a-Song Board
Story Prop Box

Beanbag Bonanza
Get Your Wiggles Out

Foam Guitar

Transition Strategy

Sing your favorite clean-up song as you walk around the room while strumming your Foam Guitar. Children will love that you are pretending to play the guitar and will get the message, in a pleasant way, that it's time to clean up. Here is a simple clean-up song to sing to the tune of "Row, Row, Row Your Boat."

> Sing, sing, sing with me.
> Sing out loud and clear,
> To tell the children everywhere,
> That clean-up time is here.

Use the guitar with your favorite clean-up song that uses children's names. As you walk around, go up to each child and encourage him to pick up the toys in his area. Invite a child who has quickly put away the toys to put on the guitar and walk around the room encouraging others to clean up.

If you play a real guitar, of course use it! Children will love the novelty of cleaning up to special music. Autoharps also can be strapped on for greater mobility and can be used in the same manner.

Variations

★ **Routine Change:** Use the guitar to "sing" other songs during routine changes throughout the day.

★ **Routine Change:** A singing reminder of where to go next along with a visual (pointing) or physical cue helps guide a child with attention deficit though the daily routine changes.

Materials

Foam sleeping-pad material (purchased through Discount School Supply—see appendix B)
Heavy cardboard
36-inch heavy shoe lace
Permanent marker or glitter glue

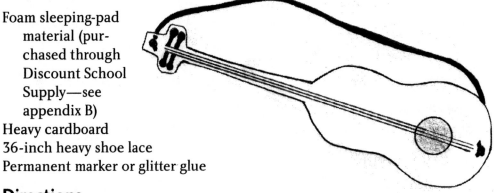

Directions

1. Enlarge the guitar shape on this page. (An easy way to enlarge it is to trace it on a transparency sheet and use an overhead projector to enlarge it to about 24 inches from tip to tip). Cut out paper pattern, trace onto foam pad, and cut out.

2. Poke one hole at the top and one hole at the base of the guitar.

3. Insert shoelace through one hole and knot it. Adjust the length of the shoelace and cut off the unneeded portion. Poke through the other hole and knot.

4. With a marker or glitter glue, add guitar features including "strings." (See illustration.)

Sensory-Sensitive Wands

Special Needs

Toddler

Transition Strategy

Wands can magically cue children when it's time to finish one activity and move to the next. All children, but especially those with specific sensory deficits (visual, auditory, or tactile), will respond to the variety of sensory materials used on these "sensory-sensitive" wands. Some of those materials might include fake fur, curling ribbons, beads, or sequined fabric. As you verbally give children one- or two-step directions to the next activity, tap them on the shoulder or brush them on their arm as an added cue. Hold a sparkly wand close by so the child with a visual disability can see.

Practically any material lends itself to becoming a wand. So be on the lookout for attractive, novel, and eye-catching items that will appeal to children and help make the transition smoother. Other things we've used include soft stuffed animals (some make a sound when you jiggle them), sponge bottle-cleaners, and attractive flyswatters. Have fun with these wands, and be creative! The following information lists materials and directions for four different wands.

Materials

Sequined fabric, any bright, shiny fabric, or fuzzy fake-
 fur fabric
Felt
Hot glue gun or sewing machine
Fiberfill
⅜-inch-diameter dowel, or tongue depressor
Poster board
Plastic beads
18-gauge wire
Curling ribbon
Masking tape

Directions

Fake Fur Wand

1.   Cut a 6-by-6-inch square from felt.

2.   Roll it into a cone shape (see illustration) and either glue or sew the seam, leaving a small hole at the bottom to insert the dowel.

3.   Trim the point off the top. Stuff the cone with fiberfill.

4.   Cut a circle of fur fabric and glue or sew to cover the top.

5.   Place glue on a dowel (12–18 inches long) and insert it in the bottom of the cone, pressing it into the filling to be sure it's securely attached. Tie ribbon on the dowel at the bottom of the cone.

Beaded Wand

1. Cut a piece of wire approximately 12 inches long.

2. Place beads in a colorful pattern on the wire. (Use masking tape temporarily to hold the first and last bead in place). Shape the wire into any shape you wish. If you choose a star, you will need a longer wire.

3. Bring the two ends together and tape them to an 18-inch-long dowel.

4. Cut about 10 pieces of brightly colored curling ribbon (about 36 inches each) and attach them with masking tape to the top of the dowel beneath the wire shape. Wrap one piece of ribbon to cover the dowel, and fasten. Curl the remaining ribbons.

Fuzzy Wand

1. Cut a 4-inch-diameter circle of fuzzy fake fur. Glue to a 4-inch-diameter poster-board circle.

2. Attach a tongue depressor and glue a blank poster-board circle on the back. This wand is great to use with toddlers because of its sensory qualities.

Sequined Wand

1. Using any shape as a pattern, cut two shiny- or sequined-fabric shapes.

2. Sew or glue the edges.

3. Stuff with fiberfill.

4. Insert a dowel and add ribbon.

Walk-Around
Schedule Board

Transition Strategy

Signal clean-up time by walking around with a schedule board. Moving close to children with this board gives them an incentive to start cleaning up. Pictures of classroom activities such as group time, snack, or outdoor play are placed on the board. A pointer directs their attention to the next activity depicted on the board. Or ask one of the children to walk around with the "schedule." Make the Walk-Around Schedule Board more versatile by adding three more surfaces: a write-and-wipe board, a song board, and an alphabet board. Directions for making the four boards are given below.

Materials

White poster board (four 22-by-28-inch sheets)
Washable markers
Clear, colored, and write-and-wipe Con-Tact paper
2 brass fasteners
Heavy cotton cording, ¼ inch thick, ½ yard long
Glue
Optional: Alphabet letters, pictures, adhesive lettering

Directions

1. Cut four circles, 22 inches in diameter, and two "pointers," 6 inches by 1 inch, from poster board.

2. Cover pointers with colored Con-Tact paper.

Schedule Board

1. On one circle, glue pictures depicting classroom activities, such as mealtime, hand washing, outdoor play, group time, and music, around the edge of the circle.

2. Cover with clear Con-Tact paper.

Write-and-Wipe Board

1. Cover another 22-inch circle with write-and-wipe Con-Tact paper.

2. You can write children's names with a transparency marker to direct their attention to clean-up or write other spontaneous messages as they are cleaning up. You can also greet them with messages at group time.

Alphabet Board

1. Place alphabet letters around the edge of another circle.

2. Cover with clear Con-Tact.

3. Attach a pointer at the center.

4. Excuse by directing the pointer at the first letter of the child's name.

Song Board

1. Cover another circle with attractive Con-Tact paper.

2. Use adhesive lettering to spell a title of a clean-up song or other song titles. (This can be changed periodically.)

3. Glue two blank sides back to back. You will have two pieces with four usable surfaces. Attach the two pieces together with 8-inch lengths of cording. (See illustration.)

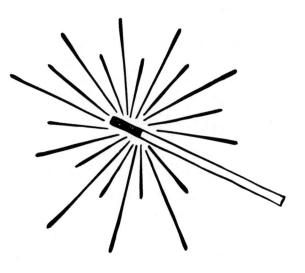

Pictorial Schedules

Transition Strategy

Help keep children focused during transitions by providing a Pictorial Schedule of the day. Children with attention-deficit disorder or cognitive delays benefit from visual cues during a transition. This handy schedule can be reviewed at the beginning of the day and used as a reminder for children who have a hard time focusing on where to go next. The individual activity cards can be rearranged as needed when your schedule changes. Individualizing the transition cues for certain children will free you up and help make them more responsible for doing the transition. It is also a good way to preview the next day's events.

Variations

★ **Routine Change:** Children who have difficulty staying on task can carry a transition stick (a 4-inch poster-board circle that has a picture of the upcoming activity, glued to a tongue depressor) to the next activity.

★ **Routine Change:** Some children are overwhelmed by stimuli when they first enter the classroom. They can wear a transition necklace, a pictorial schedule of the first two or three activities of the day, to help them focus. Simply glue pictures of these activities on an index card and attach a long ribbon to the top corners to create a necklace.

Materials

White poster board
Pictures of routines, activities, and transitions typically found in your day
    (actual photos of your children, drawings, or pictures from magazines)
Adhesive-backed Velcro strip (hook and loop), ½ yard long by ½ inch wide
Marker

Directions

1.   Count your routines, transitions, and activities that you wish to illustrate. Take or find pictures of each event.

2.   Cut poster board into 4-by-9-inch pieces, one per routine, transition, or activity.

3.   Glue pictures to poster-board pieces (one picture per card) and label each (hand washing, snack, and so on). Optional: Laminate cards.

4.   Attach the hook side of the stripping vertically or horizontally to the wall.

5.   Attach a 1-by-1-inch piece of looped strip on the back and front of each card above the illustration. (As each routine is complete, the picture can be turned over so it is blank and children can track the progression of the day's activities.)

Whale Mat

Toddler

Transition Strategy

Children settle more easily when they have a special destination! Preschoolers or toddlers will want to sit down when they get to sit on this big blue "whale." This large vinyl mat in the shape of a whale will comfortably hold you and a small group of children. Play the song "Baby Beluga" by Raffi as another motivator or cue to get children settled. The whale also makes a perfect space for you to "drop and flop" with a toddler.

Just about any shape can be used to make a sitting space for a small group of children. Match your shape to a theme or topic: a bumblebee, a dinosaur, or a flower.

Materials

4-by-5-foot piece of fabric-backed vinyl (preferably blue)
Whale pattern (see page 201)
Permanent black marker
Overhead projector
Transparency film

Directions

1. Trace the pattern on overhead transparency film.

2. Using an overhead projector, enlarge the pattern. Trace the enlarged pattern on the vinyl.

3. Use permanent marker to make the eye.

4. Cut out the whale, and it's ready to use.

Photo Key Chains

Toddler

Transition Strategy

Diaper changing is sometimes a challenging time. Keep toddlers occupied while their diapers are being changed with a set of their own plastic keys and miniature photo holder. Personalize their set of keys with their photo and a family photo. Keep the keys with their belongings or hang them on hooks above the changing table along with other children's key chains. Their key chain is easily identified and easily sanitized along with other toys. The diaper-changing routine will be a breeze.

Variation

★ **Magic Carpet Activity:** Place all of the children's family photos on a board. Attach cup hooks above each photo. Then put each child's picture in a photo holder. Children can match their photos to family photos by hanging the key chain on the cup hook.

Materials

One set of plastic keys for each child
Plastic photo holders, 2 by 3 inches, that
    can be added to a set of keys (purchased
    at discount stores in the photography
    section)
For each child, photos of the child or of the
    child's family, pets, or anything that
    interests the child
Camera and film

Directions

1. Take a photo of each child. Or, if you don't have a camera, ask parents to provide you with the photos you need.

2. Insert the photos into the picture holders and attach them to rings of keys.

3. If you wish to hang the key chains, screw coffee cup hooks into a board and mount on the wall above the changing table within easy reach.

SETTLER

Place Mat Sit-Upons

Transition Strategy

Children will settle into group time readily if they have a special seating space waiting for them. A nice variation of the traditional carpet square is the vinyl place mat, which can be found in a large variety of shapes and bright colors. You can further identify individual place mats by printing the child's name or attaching the child's picture. Children who are distractible will find an individualized destination in the group area helps them focus on where they need to be.

Variation

Make your own vinyl placemats by cutting an oval shape out of vinyl fabric (12 by 8 inches), one for each child. Using a child's photo or a page from a large, shaped notepad, such as a gingerbread boy or frog, write the child's name on the notepad paper, lay it or the photo on the mat, and cover the area with clear Con-Tact paper.

Materials

Vinyl place mat for each child
Permanent marker
Optional: Photos of children
         Clear plastic mailing tape (3 inches wide)

Directions

1. Print each child's name on a vinyl place mat.

2. If you use photos, lay them on place mats and cover with clear mailing tape or clear Con-Tact paper.

3. To reuse, remove names with hair spray. Remove pictures.

A Tub of Snakes

Transition Strategy

A tub or a box of colorful, furry snakes will surely attract children to group time! Use these stuffed snakes to bring children's attention to your next activity. Perhaps you'll read *Hide and Snake* by Keith Baker, or listen to a song about a snake, or pretend to be snakes slithering over the ground. Create a little suspense as you describe what could be in the box you've brought today. Make enough snakes so each child has one to hold during the activity. If any children are afraid of snakes, don't force them to participate until they are ready.

Variations

* **Settler:** If the snakes create unwanted behaviors (such as teasing or scaring others), introduce them as friendly snakes and offer them as a settler. The soft, furry fabric has a soothing effect on children. Let them hold the snakes while you introduce your activity or while you read your book.

* **Magic Carpet Activity:** A tub of snakes will make a good Magic Carpet activity. Children can play individually or with a buddy. They can count and sort by color or design.

Materials

Fake fur or polar-fleece fabric in bright colors (½ yard of 64-inch-wide fabric)
1 square red felt
Fabric paint—white and black
Fiberfill
Dowel or other stuffing tool

Directions

1. Make a slithery snake pattern from poster board 4 by 12 inches, keeping the snake about 3 inches wide.

2. Using a ballpoint pen, trace your pattern, side by side, across the width of the fabric. (You should get approximately 16 snakes.) Cut one tongue shape for each snake from the red felt.

3. Cut out shapes, fold each in half lengthwise with right sides together, and insert a "tongue" between the layers at one end. The part of the tongue that will show should be inside the snake at this point.

4. Sew the length of the fabric and across the tongue end, leaving the other end open. Turn right side out. The tongue should be sticking out of the end you sewed across.

5. Using a dowel, tightly stuff polyester fiberfill into the snake.

6. Sew the open end shut.

7. Draw on eyes by using white fabric paint; let dry. Make a black triangle at the center of each eye with the black paint.

tongue→

fold

Shimmering Cloth

Special Needs

Toddler

Transition Strategy

Create suspense and the element of mystery by covering an object with a shimmering sequined cloth. Young children and children with visual impairments will especially be attracted by the glittery fabric. Choose objects that will pique the interest of all the children, perhaps something with an unusual shape. Toddlers, who love hide-and-seek games, will love to find out what is under the shimmering cloth and will want you to hide it again and again.

Variation

* Use glittery fabric to sew a bag the size of a pillowcase. A drawstring is optional. Use the bag with toddlers, to hide objects. See if they can find the objects. They will love taking out the objects and putting them back in. Choose familiar items from the classroom to use in your bag.

Materials

1 yard of sequined fabric (more for larger objects)

Stickie Cube

Transition Strategy

Focus children's attention with a Stickie Cube as they settle in for your next activity. This box is covered with Con-Tact paper. Plastic-cling shapes, letters, or numbers magically stick to the outside of this box and will spark conversations with children. For older preschoolers, use alphabet letters to indicate the first letter of a child's name. "I see Nathan is sitting flat. What letter does your name start with? 'N,' that's right. I'm going to put an 'N' on the cube." Repeat. For toddlers, use simple plastic-cling objects such as a telephone, toothbrush, or umbrella, and talk about what we do with those objects. When children are settled and focused, you can flow in to your next activity.

Variations

* Instead of using plastic clings, use a write-and-wipe marker to draw pictures or print letters.

* **Extender:** Make this an interactive activity by having the children tell you a story as you put plastic-cling figures on the sides of the box. Use animals, fruits, or shapes as story visuals.

Materials

1 cube-shaped box
Write-and-wipe Con-Tact paper or static-cling sheets (purchased at office supply stores), or glossy page protectors
Scissors
Colored electrician's tape
Plastic window-cling shapes and letters (purchased from teacher supply catalogs or in discount or drug stores)
Optional: Write-and-wipe marker

Directions

1. Fill box with crumpled newspaper or fiberfill to keep it from caving in.

2. Cover the entire outside of the box with the write-and-wipe Con-Tact paper or static cling sheets.

3. Reinforce the corners with electrician's tape. See illustration.

4. Cover sides with plastic window-cling shapes or letters.

Beanbag Bonanza

Transition Strategy

The versatile beanbag! It comes in all shapes and sizes and can be used in many different ways. Use beanbags for tossing games, for passing games, and in movement activities. Use one of the many beanbag-activity audiotapes. Create some unique beanbags from discarded shower-curtain material. Filling them with aquarium rock makes them totally washable after use. Shower-curtain beanbags are great for those toddlers who like to put things in their mouths, because they are washable. Use the bags indoors or outdoors.
Safety tip: When you wash these bags, put them in a pillowcase, just in case your seams come open.

Materials

Shower-curtain fabric or vinyl liner (for shower-curtain beanbags)
Polar-fleece fabric (for polar-fleece beanbags)
Aquarium rock
Thread
Sewing machine

Directions

1. Cut shower curtain or liner into 4-by-4-inch squares.

2. With right sides together, sew two squares together, leaving a 2-inch opening on one side.

3. Turn the square right side out, and sew around the edges again (in from the edge about ⅛ inch) to reinforce the edge. Leave the hole open.

4. Fill beanbag with aquarium rock and sew shut.

5. OR, make beanbags from polar-fleece material. This fabric comes in a variety of colors and patterns. If the material has a shape such as a polar bear or a tiger, create a beanbag in that shape by cutting around the shape, allowing about ¼ inch around the outside edge; cut a second piece the same size for the back. Align the two pieces and sew around the shape, leaving a hole for filling. This beanbag doesn't have to be turned. Fill the bag with aquarium rock and sew it shut. Like the shower-curtain beanbags, these bags can be washed in the washing machine.

Get Your Wiggles Out

Transition Strategy

Anticipate when children are becoming restless and be ready with a bag of sponge shapes. Hand a sponge to each child or ask each one to pull a sponge out of the bag. Tap one child with your sponge wand to have her move into the middle of the circle. Using "dancing" music in the background, ask the child to tell about the sponge's shape, then have all the children move like that shape (for example, move like a snowflake, a leaf, or a dinosaur).

Variations

* **Extender:** Put three to five differently shaped sponges in a row. Have children shut their eyes. Take one away. Have children open their eyes as you sing the song, "Look and See" (tune: "Row, Row, Row Your Boat"): "Look, look, look and see which sponge is gone. Raise your hand if you know which sponge is gone."

Use discarded shoulder pads from blouses and sweaters, instead of sponges, for stretching activities. Children will love to use these colorful items. They can balance them on their heads, shoulders, elbows, and other body parts as they move to the music.

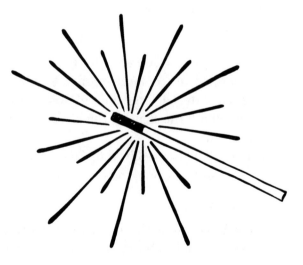

Felt-and-Velcro Hoop

Transition Strategy

This versatile prop is made with felt on one side and looped Velcro fabric on the other, so that both sides can be used by the children for storytelling, counting, sorting, and other activities. When you have a little time to spare, get out the Felt-and-Velcro Hoop and its pieces to do a flannelboard story or a counting activity with the children. The hoop is sturdy enough for children to use on their own without help from the teacher—just set the hoop out with a selection of felt pieces or counting materials that have pieces of Velcro stuck on their backs. Objects colored and cut out of heavyweight interfacing material will also stick to the felt side.

Variations

★ **Magic Carpet Activity:** Use smaller wooden embroidery hoops to make small versions of the Felt-and-Velcro Hoop. Place an assortment of mini-props in a small box such as a school supply box. Stick a small piece of Velcro to the hoop and another to the top of the box to secure the hoop to the box when not in use.

★ **Excuser:** Write each child's name on an index card, cut around the outline of the name, cover with clear Con-Tact paper, and place a small piece of Velcro on the back of the name card. Attach name cards, one by one, to the hoop to excuse children from group. Help children as necessary to recognize the letters of their names.

Materials

1 wooden quilter's hoop (30–36 inches across)
1 piece looped Velcro, large enough to cover the hoop
1 piece felt material, large enough to cover the hoop
Cording (length the same as the circumference or around the outside of
    the hoop)
Variety of felt, heavyweight interfacing, or cardboard counting or story pieces
Fabric glue or hot-glue gun

Directions

1. Place the felt and the looped Velcro together with wrong sides facing each other. Lay them over the smaller piece of the quilter's hoop.

2. Secure the material in place by fitting the larger piece of the quilter's hoop over the material and the smaller hoop. Pull the material until it is taut—it will be a snug fit.

3. Carefully cut the excess material from the edge of the hoop, leaving about ¼ inch all the way around.

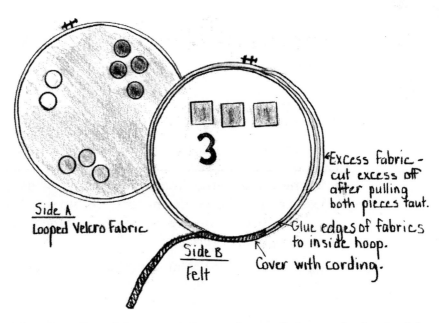

Side A
Looped Velcro Fabric

3

Side B
Felt

Excess fabric -
cut excess off
after pulling
both pieces taut.

Glue edges of fabrics
to inside hoop.

Cover with cording.

4. Glue the edge of the materials together and then to the back of the smaller hoop.

5. Glue cording around the edge of the hoop, covering the edge of the material.

Versatile Tri-Fold Board

Transition Strategy

Do you need some quick activities to extend your group time? Pull out this all-in-one activity board. This versatile board is designed to involve children in a variety of activities, from matching, to drawing, to telling stories. Each side is covered with a different texture or surface. You can easily switch to other activities, because everything is right there with the board. Create the following six board surfaces:

★ Clear vinyl pocket for holding papers such as pictures or recipes or for attaching plastic clings
★ Looped Velcro fabric surface for attaching hooked Velcro stripping pieces
★ Felt surface for attaching felt pieces
★ Solid-color Con-Tact paper surface with hooked fastener stripping along each side
★ Envelopes to hold craft sticks
★ Solid-color or printed Con-Tact surface

Ways to use this board are endless, but here are a few suggestions:

★ Use the looped fabric or felt surfaces to tell stories.
★ Sets of matching pictures can be used with the hook and loop strips on Con-Tact paper. Let the children connect the matching pictures with a transparency marker. Wipe off the marker, change the matching pictures, and try again.

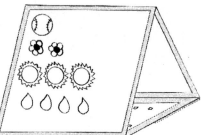

★ Children can participate in counting, sorting, sequencing, or matching activities using the envelopes. Each envelope has a piece of hooked strip on the front, and numerals or shapes can be attached. Children can count craft sticks to match the numeral and slip them in the envelope. Or they can match a corresponding shape. This section of the board can be changed to reflect the learning that's taking place in the classroom.

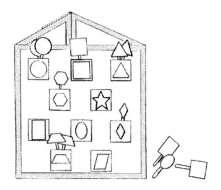

★ Pin a piece of construction paper to the Con-Tact surface with clothespins and let children draw with markers or crayons.

Materials

Eleven 18-by-18-inch squares of heavyweight cardboard
Piece of looped Velcro fabric, 18 by 18 inches

Solid-color or printed Con-Tact paper, 2 yards
Clear Con-Tact paper, 1/2 yard
Piece of clear vinyl, 18 by 18 inches
Piece of felt or stiffened felt, 18 by 18 inches
20 pieces of adhesive-backed hooked Velcro stripping,
    1 inch by 1 inch each
6-inch strip of inch-wide adhesive-backed hook-and-loop fastener
10 white letter-size envelopes
55 craft sticks
2 heavy-duty plastic sandwich bags or quart-size self-closing bags
Colored duct tape or clear plastic mailing tape
Spray adhesive
Rubber cement
Scissors
Utility knife
2 spring clothespins
Additional pieces of felt, hooked Velcro stripping pieces, and plastic, for
    making shapes, numbers, and storyboard pieces

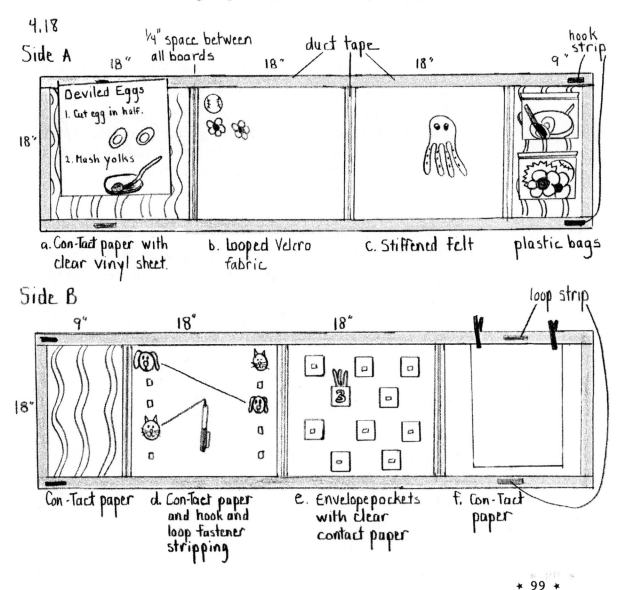

Directions

1. Cut cardboard into 11 squares, 18 by 18 inches each. To make a sturdy board, layer and glue 3 pieces of cardboard together to make one square. Repeat two more times so that you have three sturdy boards. Cut the remaining 2 squares in half and layer the 4 pieces together to make a support flap for the end of the tri-fold board. You should end up with 3 squares (6 surfaces to work with) and 1 rectangle support flap.

2. Prepare each 18-by-18-inch surface as follows:

    a. Adhere solid or printed Con-Tact paper, and then tape an 18-by 18-inch piece of clear vinyl to the board, leaving one edge open, so you can insert pictures.

    b. Attach looped Velcro fabric with a spray adhesive.

    c. Attach felt fabric with a spray adhesive.

    d. Adhere solid-colored Con-Tact paper, then add 5 pieces of adhesive-backed hooked Velcro stripping along each side (see illustration) for holding numerals, shapes, color shapes, and matching pieces attached with looped strips.

    e. Attach 10 letter-size envelopes with rubber cement, then cover the board with clear Con-Tact paper (see illustration 4.18), providing access to the envelopes by cutting slits with a utility knife.

    f. Cover with solid or printed Con-Tact paper.

3. Place 2 prepared squares together with the treated side facing out. Tape all four edges of each square using 3-inch duct tape or plastic mailing tape by folding it over the edge. Repeat this step two more times for the squares and once for the support flap. This should give you three two-sided sections and the support flap.

4. With someone's help, join the 4 sections with duct tape. Space the boards about ¼ inch apart.

5. On the 9-by-18-inch support piece, attach two plastic sandwich bags or quart-size self-closing bags to store pieces for the activities (transparency markers, craft sticks, and so on).

6. Attach Velcro strips along the edge of the support piece and the bottom square (see illustration) to hold the board in place when folded.

Sing-a-Song Board

Transition Strategy

A nice way to review old songs children know, and a good way to extend an activity, is by using a song board. Create several song boards to have on hand for when you have a few minutes to fill! Each song board has easily recognized illustrations of the children's favorite songs, such as "Five Little Monkeys," "This Old Man," and "Who Stole the Cookie?" Ask a child to come up, select a song on the board, and name the song. He will be able to "read" the words because the picture is right there, reinforcing a nice prereading skill. That child or another can use the pretend microphone to lead the group in singing the song. Sing as many songs as needed to fill the time.

Variation

★ **Magical Moment:** A smaller, hand-held version of the song board can go with you when you are on the move with children, down the hall or on a field trip. Put the boards on rings to keep them together.

Materials

Poster board, 28 by 30 inches
Markers
Song or finger-play pictures, such as a wagon for "Little Red Wagon" or a clock for "Hickory Dickory Dock"
Optional: Toy microphone

Directions

1. Select songs and finger plays that are familiar to the children.

2. Enlarge song illustrations on a copy machine and cut them out to create silhouettes. Then place visuals on the poster board and trace around them. Add a few features to each silhouette, such as spokes in the tires, so the shape is easily recognized by children.

3. Write the title of the song or finger play within each silhouette.

Story Prop Box

Transition Strategy

A Story Prop Box is another clever way to hold children's attention when you have a little lag time between activities. Many children's stories lend themselves to storytelling with props. One such story is *Mouse Count*, by Ellen Stoll Walsh. (Other books that would make good story boxes are *Caps for Sale*, by Esphyr Slobodkina, *The Very Hungry Caterpillar*, by Eric Carle, *If You Give a Mouse a Cookie*, by Laura Joffe Numeroff, or *Mouse Paint*, by Ellen Stoll Walsh.) Create or gather pieces—stuffed mice, a stuffed snake, rocks—and store them in a decorated box (your Story Prop Box). Become familiar with the story—familiar enough to tell it rather than read it. This allows you to adjust the length of the story. Children will enjoy this quick story, and the visuals will help hold their attention. They can even help tell the story. From time to time, add props for a new story to the box.

Variation

* Make your story box into a song box. Put in props that go with children's favorite songs. Try including props for "The Old Lady Who Swallowed a Fly," "Apples and Bananas," or the peanut-butter song.

Materials

A sturdy box with a cover
Patterned Con-Tact paper
Mouse Count, by Ellen Stoll Walsh
Mouse Count story-box props:
    A stuffed snake or a fake snake
    A rock

Materials for making mice:

Gray or brown felt
Movable eyes
Scissors
Fabric glue
Twine
Small pom-poms

Directions for box

1. Cover the box with attractive Con-Tact paper.

2. Using the patterns, make 10 mice. Cut two bodies and one ear piece per mouse.

3. Make two slits in one body piece, as shown on the pattern.

4. Pull the ear piece through the slits. This is the top piece.

5. Attach the twine tail to the wide end of the body piece and glue the top piece to a flat body piece.

6. To make the face, glue 2 movable eyes and a small pom-pom to the pointed end of the body .

7. Place all the props in the box.

8. Familiarize yourself with the story, and practice using the props before you perform for the children.

Actual-Size
Mouse Body

Actual-Size
Mouse Ears

Place-Mat Puzzles

Special Needs

Toddler

Transition Strategy

Use vinyl place mats to create a variety of floor puzzles that children can pull out when they are waiting for the other children to finish up the previous activity or routine. Make them simple (two or three pieces) to difficult (twelve to fifteen pieces), so that they meet the developmental levels of all your children. Place-Mat Puzzles are ideal for toddlers because they are simple and easily sanitized. Choose place-mat designs that appeal to children's interests, such as a movie theme ("Lion King") or kitties and puppies.

Variation

★ Cut several different shapes from one or more place mats. These cut nicely on a stencil-cutting machine (see appendix B). After the shapes are cut, then cut each one in half, varying the pattern (zigzag, wavy, diagonal, and so on). Mix all the halves up and have children find the matches.

Materials

Vinyl place mats (a variety of designs)
Paper cutter or scissors
Self-closing plastic storage bags (1-gallon size)
Permanent marker

Directions

1. Purchase place mats, preferably on sale or at garage sales.

2. Cut mats into pieces using a paper cutter or scissors. You can cut straight or curvy lines and vary the number of pieces for each mat. This will add to the range of difficulty.

3. Store in self-closing storage bags on your Magic Carpet shelf to be used only at special times.

Hint: Number the back of each puzzle piece with permanent marker, assigning a new number for each puzzle. This will help tremendously with clean-up, should several puzzles be out at the same time.

Magnetic Board with Pieces

Transition Strategy

Provide a magnetic board with magnetic numbers and letters or collect refrigerator magnets that lend themselves to matching, sorting, and classifying, such as animal faces or different colors of magnets. Gather magnetic pieces that are interesting and will appeal to your age group. For toddlers, make sure pieces are large enough to be used safely. Children can easily and quickly pick up this activity and work either individually or with a buddy. The resistance of the magnet on the metal surface is even a learning experience for them!

Materials

12-by-16-inch metal stovetop burner cover, or a metal board used by cross stitchers, or a metal cookie sheet

A variety of interesting refrigerator magnets and magnetic numbers and letters

For making your own magnets:

Adhesive-backed magnetic strip (available in craft stores)
File folders or poster board
Con-Tact paper

Directions

Making Your Own Magnets

1.   Cut out numbers or shapes from file folders or poster board.

2.   Cover pieces with Con-Tact paper.

3.   Place a small piece of adhesive-backed magnetic strip on the back of each piece.

Sticker Match

Special Needs

Toddler

Transition Strategy

This sticker-match game can be used individually or with a friend. With the handy marker, buddies can take turns matching stickers that are on the sticker board. When all the stickers are matched with the write-and-wipe marker, the lines can be wiped off and used again and again. Choose stickers that appeal to children's interests and have several sticker match boards available, as this will be a popular choice.

Variations

★ Use vinyl place mats to create matching games for children. Purchase plain vinyl place mats and interesting stickers. You will need two of each sticker. Arrange one set of stickers in a line across the top of the place mat and the matching set of stickers in a different order across the bottom. On the back attach a self-closing bag in which you place a write-and-wipe marker and a tissue. Children match the stickers by drawing lines between them. When finished, children can erase the lines and try the next matching game. Make several place-mat matching games, varying the difficulty by changing the number of stickers to be matched and the amount of detail in the stickers.

★ **Magical Moment:** A smaller version of the sticker-match board can be used as a Magical Moment when you're waiting for the bus.

Materials

Two poster boards, 28 by 30 inches each
Stickers (two sets usually come in a package and have 10–12 designs)
Watercolor marker
Small piece of elastic
Clear Con-Tact paper

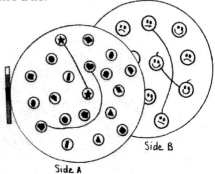

Side A
Side B

Directions

1. Cut two large circles, using the full poster board.

2. Randomly cover one side of one circle with pairs of stickers, mixing up the pairs.

3. Repeat step 2 on the other circle. For toddlers or for children with cognitive delay, reduce the number of stickers to be matched; make the game more challenging for children who do this type of activity well.

4. Cover the sticker side with clear Con-Tact paper (cut a little larger than the circles); snip the edges and fold them over.

5. Attach a loop of elastic—just enough to fit a marker—to one edge and staple. Insert the marker for handy access.

6. Glue the two circles together back to back.

I Spy You

Transition Strategy

Avert restless waiting behaviors by providing children with a photo collage to look at while they wait. Post it by the washroom door, so children can look for pictures of themselves and others. Encourage them to talk about what they were doing when the pictures were taken. This is a great language activity and makes waiting time enjoyable.

Variations

★ Create a collage using miscellaneous stickers instead of photos. Adjust the size of the poster board based on how many stickers you have. Use both sides of the poster board. This is a great way to keep children occupied as they look for a specific sticker, and then another, and another.

★ Calendar Picture Collage—Look for calendars that have thumbnail pictures of each month's calendar photo on the back page. Cut out these small photos and combine them with other calendar thumbnail pictures into one big collage. This will keep children interested and occupied as they wait for their friends.

★ Create a calendar matching board by mounting calendar pictures and the thumbnail pictures in random order. See if children can find the big and little pictures that match.

Materials

Camera and film, or photos of children engaged in a variety of classroom
    activities, or photos of family activities provided by the families
Poster board (24 by 28 inches)
Rubber cement or spray adhesive
Clear Con-Tact paper

Directions

1. Take photos of your classroom activities or ask parents to provide pictures of family activities.

2. Adjust size of poster board according to how many pictures you have.

3. Cut around the main focus of each picture, discarding the background. Create a collage of pictures and attach with rubber cement or spray adhesive to the poster board. For a true collage effect, fit pictures together in a way that leaves no white spaces.

4. Cover with clear Con-Tact paper to protect.

Colorful Water Ring

Transition Strategy

Children love the mesmerizing flow of water through the clear plastic tubing. Toddlers will especially enjoy watching water flow, and the colorful water ring provides extra entertainment by adding glittery objects to the mix. Children love to carry the rings around and sit on them. Use a ring while you are waiting with children or give one to a child who is waiting after a diaper change or dressing for outdoors. A child can use the ring as a soothing object at naptime. Have several of them available.

Variation

* For a different effect, fill the tube with colored water and mineral or baby oil.

Materials

One yard of plastic tubing, between ¼-inch and 1-inch diameter (found in local hardware stores)
One connector (same size as the tubing)
Tap water
Plastic confetti, plastic beads, glitter—anything eye-catching and colorful

Directions

1. Place the connector into one end of the tubing.

2. Put beads, glitter, confetti and other objects into the tube.

3. Fill the tube with warm water, leaving a little air space so water can move through the tube. The warm water makes the tubing more pliable and thus easier to push onto the connector.

4. Push the open end of the tube onto the free end of the connector so the tube forms a ring.

5. To change contents, run hot water over the connector to release it from the tube.

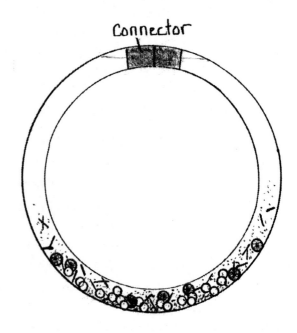

Connector

Accordion Photo Boards

Transition Strategy

The Accordion Photo Board is a homemade photo foldout book. It will be very popular with all children. It folds up so it can be easily stored and brought out when needed, and it's small enough that children can hold it. Use it when toddlers are on the changing table. Set it on the back of the changing table so that children can look at the pictures as they participate in this routine. An enlarged version of the Accordion Photo Board is great to use with older toddlers. Keep a basket of the boards by the potty chair or near the group area. Change the pictures often to hold children's attention.

Variations

* **Attention Grabber:** Use the larger accordion board at group time. Pictures are easily changed to match the interests of the children or a current topic, such as grandpas and grandmas, or gardens.

* Make a larger accordion board by using 9-by-12-inch plastic page protectors instead of photo pockets. Change the dimensions of the Con-Tact paper and poster board to adjust for the larger size. Assemble using the directions below. Enlarge photos of children to 8 by 10 inches on a color copier (available at many office-supply or copy centers). Mount pictures on the poster-board pieces and slip them into the plastic page protectors. Use spray adhesive to attach to the board. This accordion board can be hung on the wall in front of the potty chair.

Materials

Con-Tact paper
Clear plastic photo pockets (4 by 6 inches) or photo album pages, cut apart
Poster board
Photos or calendar pictures

Directions

1. Cut 5-by-8-inch pieces from poster board or use 5-by-8-inch index cards (5 pieces will accommodate 10 photos).

2. Cut two lengths of Con-Tact paper (approximately 43 by 6 inches for 5 pieces of cardboard).

3. Remove paper backing and lay the pieces of cardboard on the Con-Tact paper approximately ½ inch apart. Cover with the second piece of Con-Tact paper.

4. On the outside of each section, attach a photo pocket. If it doesn't come with adhesive, use spray adhesive to attach to the board.

5. Slip close-up photos of the children in each pocket.

Peek-a-Boo and Pop-Up Cards

Transition Strategy

Are you looking for a transitional prop that is easy to carry when you take children out of the room? Try tucking several small Peek-a-Boo and Pop-Up Cards in your pocket or fanny pack. Peek-a-Boo Cards have a cut-out flap on the front that hides a picture beneath it. Read the clues that are written on the flap and encourage children to guess what or who is inside. Here are a couple of riddles to write on the flap: "I'm built when it's cold. I am usually round. Sometimes I a wear a hat. I melt when it's warm." Inside the card is a picture of a snow-person. Or, "I'm a boy. I'm five years old. I like to draw and play basketball. I'm in kindergarten." Inside is a picture of a child in your class. Children love riddles, making this an easy way to keep children occupied while waiting for others. Pop-Up Cards open up to reveal pictures of the children or favorite stickers.

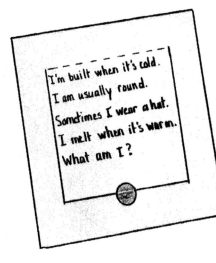

Variations

★ **Extender:** Ask a child to select a card and read the riddle. The pictures on the cards can extend the theme you are currently using.

★ **Excuser:** Make Peek-a-Boo Cards for all of the children in your class. Simply write their names on the flaps. When it's time to excuse children, select a Peek-a-Boo Card from a basket. Hold it up and see if the child can identify the name. Give clues if children are too young for name recognition.

Materials

Colored file folders
Clear Con-Tact paper
Pictures of children or of things familiar to children, or stickers
A stencil-cutting machine (see appendix B)
Markers
Utility knife
Scissors
Tape

Directions

Peek-a-Boo Cards

1. Cut file folders into 10-by-5-inch pieces.

2. Laminate, or cover both sides with clear Con-Tact paper.

3. Use the stencil-cutting machine to cut the peek-a-boo flap (see illustration on previous page).

4. Select a picture, sticker, or photo and tape it inside. Write a riddle to go with the picture.

Pop-Up Cards

1. Cut file folders into 10-by-5-inch pieces and laminate them.

2. Use the stencil-cutting machine to cut the pop-up slits.

3. With card folded, make two 1-inch cuts from the fold, ½ inch apart (see illustration below).

4. Repeat step 2 twice more, to make 6 cuts. These cuts can be of varying lengths.

5. Bend where you stop cutting, and fold into Pop-Up Card. Open up, and on the inside strips glue pictures, stickers, or photos of the children.

Quiet-As-a-Mouse Puppet

Transition Strategy

Tuck a little mouse puppet in your pocket and tell children that you have a special visitor who will whisper in their ears to excuse them today. Pull out your mouse finger puppet and "walk" it to a child. Whisper in that child's ear to get her jacket and backpack. Children will eagerly wait for the mouse puppet to come and whisper in their ears!

Variations

* **Routine Change:** Use the mouse puppet to cue children from one activity to another. Go to each child with your mouse puppet and whisper in her ear what to pick up: "I'd like you to pick up three blocks." Or use the puppet to tell children where they are going next when they have picked up the blocks.

* **Magical Moment:** Keep the mouse handy in your pocket. Slip it out when you need to get children's attention or to help you sing or say a finger play with the children. They will be intrigued when the mouse whispers to them.

Materials

Gray or brown felt
Pink felt
Movable eyes
Small pom-poms
Glue

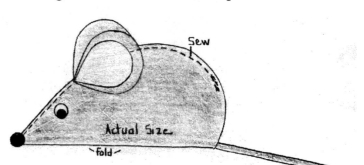

Directions

1. From gray or brown felt, cut a heart shape (approximately 4 inches) for the mouse's body, a smaller heart shape for the ear, and a thin strip for the tail.

2. Cut a smaller heart shape from pink felt for the inside of the ear.

3. Glue pink heart on small gray heart to make the ear.

4. Fold large heart in half. Place the ear near the point and sew from the nose end to the back, catching the point of the ear in the seam and leaving the back open for your finger. Attach the tail to the back. Optional: Glue the seams instead of sewing.

5. Glue the movable eyes and pom-pom nose to the pointed end of the mouse puppet.

Write-and-Wipe Cube

Transition Strategy

Reinforce children's letter-recognition skills at the same time you are excusing them from the group. Use a Write-and-Wipe Cube and its handy pen to write children's names or initials (depending on their skill level) as the signal that they are excused. Marks on the Write-and-Wipe Cube are easily erased. Or use the pen to write names of colors to indicate that all children wearing that color are excused.

Materials

A sturdy cube (6 inches is a nice size)
Write-and-wipe Con-Tact paper (found in school supply stores or conference exhibits)
A washable transparency pen
Adhesive-backed loop-and-hook fastener strip
Colored masking tape or electrician's tape

Directions

1. Cut write-and-wipe Con-Tact paper to cover all six sides of box.

2. Reinforce all the corners and cover up the seams by using colored electrician's tape.

3. Attach a small piece of hooked fastener strip to the transparency pen and adhere the looped piece to the edge of the box.

Excuse Me Photo Cube

Transition Strategy

A novel way to excuse children at the end of the day is to use a photo cube. With pictures of the children in the photo pockets on each side of the cube, roll it on the floor. The child whose picture lands facing up is excused. If you have more than six children, include additional pictures in each photo pocket. As each child is excused, remove that picture, leaving the next one in view. Children will attentively wait to see if they will be next. It's easy to change pictures, which renews their attention.

Variations

★ **Routine Change:** Give the photo cube to children while they are having their diapers changed. Let them manipulate the box while doing this routine.

★ **Settler:** Hold up the cube when the child arrives at group. Give that child an individual minute and recognition.

Materials

Small cube-shaped box, large enough to attach 4-by-6-inch photos
Plastic packaging tape
Printed or colored Con-Tact paper
Clear plastic photo pockets (from office supply stores)
Photos of the children in your group

Directions

1. Cover the entire box with Con-Tact paper.

2. Use plastic packaging tape to reinforce the corners.

3. Attach the clear plastic photo pockets to each side of your box.

4. Slip a child's photo into each pocket.

5

Sensational Senses

ROUTINE CHANGES
Clean-Up Rap
Beat the Clock
Glow-in-the-Dark Megaphone
Follow the Light
Pass the Beanbag

SETTLERS
Weighted Fleece Bags
Gigantic Letters
Song-Riddles
Hanky Baby
Sensory Soothers

EXCUSERS
Count the Steps
Twirling Ribbon Wand

MAGICAL MOMENTS
Teacher Pockets
See-Through Crayons
Musical Pictures
Bubbles on the Go
Mini Microphone

ATTENTION GRABBERS
Smile Sticks
Stuffed Animal Wand

MAGIC CARPET ACTIVITIES
Scrubber Puzzles
3-D Snow-Person
Water Pillows
Folder of Flowers
Box-o-Books
Mini Sound Shakers

EXTENDERS
"Toddlers Like To" Book
Move-Your-Body Cube
Color Cards
Where Is the Animal?
Emotions Song

STRETCHERS
Sponge Balls
Tube Roller
Mirroring
Streamers on a Hoop
Balloon on a Ring
Shape-Up Aerobics

Clean-Up Rap

Transition Strategy

Children are drawn to any directions that are sung to them. Raps have a natural rhythm that children will be drawn to, and you will find them "rapping" right along with you as they clean the room in no time at all. A rap is similar to a chant, only with a definite beat and rhythm, and usually a faster speed. Create your own rap with the help of the children, or pick one from the following samples:

Sample I:

> It's clean-up time, it's clean-up time.
> Let's all do our share.
> Look under the table, look under the chair.
> Hey everybody, lend a hand, help us out and do what you can.
> The blocks need stacking, the Legos put away.
> Come on everybody, it's the end of the day.

Sample II:

> It's clean-up time around the room.
> We don't need fancy tools.
> Just use your hands, your eyes, your ears.
> And our room will be clean and clear.

Sample III:

> We had fun playing today, now it's time to put the toys away.
> Chorus: Clean up who, clean up you, we don't need any boo-boo's.
> Put our toys where they go, it keeps our room nice you know.
> Chorus: Clean up who, clean up you, we don't need any boo-boo's.
> We did a good job, yes we did, hooray for us, hooray for us kids.
> Chorus: Clean up who, clean up you, we don't need any boo-boo's.

Sample IV:

> Clap your hands and stomp your feet.
> Let's make our room clean and neat.
> If we put our things away, we will have a better day.
> Clean-up time is for us.
> Clean-up time is a must.
> This is our clean-up song.
> We can use it all day long.

ROUTINE
CHANGE

Beat the Clock

Special Needs

Transition Strategy

When clean-up time becomes tedious and difficult for your children, set a timer. Children love to play "beat the clock." Setting a timer for children to "beat" will spur them to move quickly to get those toys picked up or get coats off and hung in cubbies. Choose either a bell-type kitchen timer or an hourglass that must be watched rather than listened for. When using a timer for clean-up time, it is recommended that you first set guidelines with the children to encourage children to put toys away with care and not simply throw things onto shelves in order to beat the timer. The bell, along with one or two specific clean-up directions, will help highly distractible children stay on task. Set the timer for a realistic amount of time (five minutes to start), so that children can experience success quickly. Each time you do this, decrease the time by thirty seconds to increase the challenge. Keep decreasing the time just a little until you get clean-up time back to your desired amount of time. Note: Children's interest in this transition activity is usually short-lived, but it's very effective in re-sparking children's interest in clean-up time for a short while.

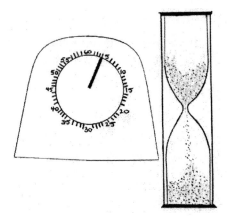

Variation

★ **Settler:** As children transition from activities in which they finish at different times (such as snack) and move into group time, give them a basket of books. They can sit quietly on the floor to read alone or with one or two friends. When the last child is almost done, set the timer for one or two minutes to let the children know they have that much time to finish up the book they are reading.

Glow-in-the-Dark Megaphone

Special Needs

Transition Strategy

Make a little magic happen when you turn off the lights to signal a change in the schedule. Use this small Glow-in-the-Dark Megaphone to announce clean-up time, and every child in your classroom will have their eyes on you and their ears listening. If you normally turn off the lights to signal clean-up time for the children, adding the Glow-in-the-Dark Megaphone will give more emphasis to their sense of sight and encourage children to focus on you and listen more carefully. Megaphones allow you to speak a little more loudly so you can be heard over the noise in the room without shouting.

Variation

★ **Excuser:** Dim the lights and use the Glow-in-the-Dark Megaphone when it's time to excuse children from group time or to go home for the day. Move to stand near each child as you announce his name. The children will be fascinated watching the megaphone move from child to child and will wait patiently for it to come to them. The added visual of something that glows in the dark will make listening much easier.

Materials

Heavy-duty cardboard tube (same size as a paper-towel tube)
Glow-in-the-dark paint, stickers, or tape

Directions

1. Paint the cardboard tube with the glow-in-the-dark contact paint.
2. Or, cover the tube with colored Con-Tact paper and decorate it with lots of glow-in-the-dark stickers or tape.

Follow the Light

Transition Strategy

There is something about flashlights that children, especially toddlers, are drawn to. Appeal to the children's sense of sight when it's time to change activities by using a normal flashlight. You can lead the way to the next activity either by flashing the light on the area or props for the activity, or by physically leading the way with the children following you and your flashlight beam. Dim the lights in the room and shine a flashlight on the next activity while you give simple directions. This will help cut down on other distractions around the room and will help children focus on what is being said. This is great for children who are easily distracted. You can decorate a simple flashlight with stickers to match the topic being done at the time.

Variation

* **Settler:** Flash the light on the body of a child and say, "I see Susie is ready to start the group." The children will quickly get ready for group, eagerly waiting for the light to shine on them. Or to excuse children from the group without using words, tell the children that when the light shines on them, they can move to the next activity.

Materials

Flashlight(s)
Optional: stickers

Directions

If desired, place stickers on the outside of the flashlight handle.

ROUTINE
CHANGE

Pass the Beanbag

Transition Strategy

If you have times in your schedule when children have to stand in line and wait, such as in a lunch line, be prepared with this game. Hand a beanbag over your shoulder to the first person in line. He passes the beanbag over his shoulder to the next person in line. Each person imitates the motion of the previous person. You can vary the movements by passing the beanbag through your legs, or twisting to the right or left. The movement, and the sensory aspect of this game, will help children focus their attention and will make the time pass quickly while waiting.

Variations

★ **Excuser:** When it's time to go home for the day, have children excuse each other. While they sit in a circle, softly call one child's name. Gently toss the beanbag to that child. That child calls out another child's name, gently tosses that child the beanbag, and then leaves the group. This continues until all the children have left.

★ **Excuser:** Try this tip to encourage children to get coats on and get ready to go quickly. While one teacher helps children zip coats and gather backpacks, the other teacher can watch for children who are ready to go. When a child is ready, the second teacher says, "I see Joey is ready to go home," and tosses a beanbag to Joey. Continue tossing beanbags until all children have a beanbag to hold. Manipulating the beanbags while they wait stimulates their senses and keeps their hands occupied. Then when it's time to get on the bus or leave with a parent, children are excused one at a time. On the way out the door, they toss the beanbag either back to the teacher or into a decorated basket or box. The children will have great fun trying to "make a basket."

SETTLER

Weighted Fleece Bags

Transition Strategy

Weighted Fleece Bags are excellent for children who have sensory integration problems, attention-deficit disorder, or trouble settling down. As children gather for group, give them weighted bags that they can drape around the backs of their necks, across their arms, or simply in their laps. The sensation of weight calms them down and helps them focus. The soft texture of the fabric is also very soothing. All of your children may want to try these weighted bags, and if the bags help them as well, all the better. The nice thing about these bags is that they can be laundered.

Variations

★ Heat these bags in the microwave or in the clothes dryer for 1–2 minutes. The warmth of the bag is additionally soothing to children, and bags stay warm for a surprisingly long time.

★ Use your imagination and cut polar-fleece fabric in squares or other shapes to make a variety of bags.

Materials

Polar-fleece fabric
Aquarium rock
Sewing machine

Directions

1. Enlarge the shape at the left to approximately 14 by 5 inches on a piece of cardboard.

2. Using this as your pattern, trace the shape on polar-fleece fabric. Fold the fabric and sew on the traced line, leaving an open space an inch long.

3. Cut around the outside edge approximately ¼ inch from the stitching.

4. Fill with aquarium rock and sew shut.

pattern for neck bag

SETTLER

Gigantic Letters

Transition Strategy

Having something to look at will help children focus on what is being said while they are settling into group time. Gigantic Letters are a versatile prop that can be used in a variety of ways during these times. Have the first letter of each child's name on hand as the children come to group time. As they are getting settled, hold up one letter at a time and sing the following song with each child's name (to the *Sesame Street* tune).

> J is for Jenny, that's good enough for me.
> J is for Jenny, that's good enough for me.
> J is for Jenny, that's good enough for me.
> Oh Jenny, Jenny, Jenny starts with J.

Or, sing a HELLO song, having five children hold up one gigantic letter each, spelling out the word HELLO. Using the same tune as above, sing:

> Hello children, I'm glad that you are here.
> Hello children I'm glad that you are here.
> Hello children I'm glad that you are here.
> Oh hello, hello, hello everyone.

Variations

* **Excuser:** Hold up one letter at a time and say, "If your name starts with ___, you can go to (destination)." Emphasize the letter's sound as you say this—for example, "If your name starts with buh, buh, B...."

* **Excuser:** Make the letters for the word GOODBYE. Substitute for HELLO in the above song. "Good-bye children, I'm glad that you were here . . ." As you sing the song and children hold the letters, you can tap children to leave group time. Finish this transition by collecting the letters from the children and setting the letters aside as you sing the song one more time.

Materials

Poster board
Decorative or clear Con-Tact paper
12-inch letter stencils

Directions

1. Using the stencils, trace each letter of the alphabet onto poster board. Cut out.

2. Cover the letters with Con-Tact paper.

SETTLER

Song-Riddles

Transition Strategy

While children are getting settled into group time or waiting for an activity to begin, sing a Song-Riddle to help them sharpen their listening and thinking skills. To the tune of "The Muffin Man," make up songs about the children in your group such as

Oh do you know a boy who's four, a boy who's four, a boy who's four
Oh do you know a boy who's four, and he's wearing a red shirt today.

The last line in the song can be changed to meet the developmental level of your children—for example, "...and whose name is (child's name)" for toddlers, or "...and whose name begins with (initial)" for older preschoolers.

Variations

★ **Extender:** This same transition technique can be used to extend a group time, or during Magical Moments.

★ **Excuser:** To excuse children from group times, sing the song as follows:

If you are a boy with a green shirt, a green shirt, a green shirt,
If you are a boy with a green shirt, you can go outside.

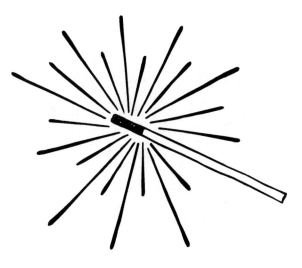

Hanky Baby

Transition Strategy

For a unique prop to help children get settled, make each child in your class a Hanky Baby. These cute little babies made from hankies are great for holding onto gently during group time or even while riding on the bus. Tell the children they are babies that need to be held gently and quietly. This is sure to calm even the most active child in your class.

Materials

White or ivory man's handkerchief (16-inch square)
Small amount polyester stuffing
⅛-inch-wide satin ribbon (approximately 20 inches long)
½-inch-wide lace (approximately 6 inches long)
Optional: small satin rose
Optional: baby powder
Craft glue

Directions

1. Fold one side of the handkerchief about 7 inches in from the edge.

2. Place the ball of stuffing in the middle of the fold. If desired, sprinkle a pinch of baby powder on the stuffing to stimulate the sense of smell. Gather up the hanky around the stuffing to become the head. Secure by tying with the satin ribbon.

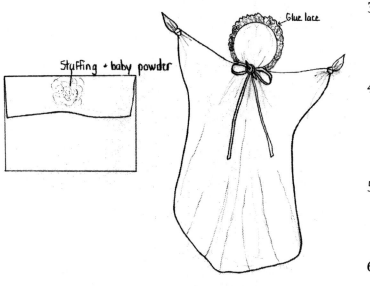

3. Glue the piece of lace around the center of the head to look like the edge of a bonnet (see illustration).

4. To make the arms, knot the corners of the handkerchief that are just below the head. Leave about 1 inch sticking out to make the hands.

5. Tie the ribbon around the neck into a small bow. Glue the rose into the center of the bow, if desired.

6. You could also make these babies out of novelty material that matches the topic you are doing in your classroom at the time, such as material with hearts or snowflakes. Cut the material into 16½-inch squares. To finish the edges, fold over ¼ inch, iron, and sew. Continue with the steps above.

SETTLER

Sensory Soothers

Transition Strategy

Having something to manipulate in their hands is very soothing for children of all ages. It is particularly useful for children with sensory integration difficulties, very active children, and toddlers. A wide range of sensory toys is available (see list and directions below) to use for this purpose. Decorate a special canister or tub and fill it with sensory toys. Have it available for group time. Let children choose a toy and hold it throughout group time or book time. Besides calming a child, it will occupy her hands and help her keep her hands by her own body.

Materials

Large metal popcorn canister or other large storage container
Decorative Con-Tact paper
Permanent marker
Variety of sensory toys:
    Koosh-brand balls
    Foam stress balls (also come in a variety of shapes)
    Flour or salt-filled balloons (see directions below)
    Small stuffed animals
    Nylon body-wash balls
    Bottles filled with oil and water

Directions

Container

1.   Cover container with decorative Con-Tact paper.

2.   With permanent marker write words—TOY BOX—on outside.

3.   Fill with sensory toys.

Flour or Salt Balloon

1.   Use large, heavy balloons. You can double up the balloons to reinforce and prevent possible accidents.

2.   Insert a small funnel into the opening of a balloon.

3.   Spoon flour or salt into the balloon, packing it down through the outside of the balloon as you fill.

4.   Double-knot the end, leaving as little air space inside the balloon as possible.

Note: Do NOT use this sensory soother if you have any children who are allergic to latex.

Smile Sticks

Transition Strategy

These Smile Sticks are sure to add fun to your day and create lots more smiles. Whenever you want to get the children's attention quickly and quietly (during group time, on a field trip, or when getting ready to go outside), simply grab a Smile Stick out of your pocket, hold it up to your face, and start talking. All eyes and ears will soon be on you, intrigued by the appearance of your new smile, and therefore your new look! For added fun, say the following finger play. While you chant the finger play, hand a Smile Stick to a child at the start of each verse and have him do the actions in the finger play (wave "hello," laugh "tee-hee, tee-hee, tee-hee," hop, and so on).

"Five Friendly Girls and Boys"

One little smiling child, wondering what to do,
(S)he waved "hello" to a friend, then there were two!
Two silly children laughing, Tee-hee, tee-hee, tee-hee,
Along came another giggler, then there were three!
Three grinning children, hopping on the floor,
Another came to join them, then there were four!
Four happy children, doing a hand jive,
One more came clapping, so then there were five!
Five happy girls and boys, making a joyful, playful noise!

Variation

* Create Smile Sticks using photos of the real smiles of the children in your classroom. Scan pictures of the children with a computer scanner. Enlarge a child's smile and make a copy of just this enlarged area. Glue the photocopy onto poster board or a file folder. Trace the smile shape on the next page over the picture, centering the smile within the shape. Cut out the shape and cover it with clear Con-Tact paper.

Materials

Tongue depressors
Poster board or file folder
Clear Con-Tact paper
Markers
Glue

Directions

1. Trace and cut the smile shape out of poster board or a file folder.

2. Draw a wide smile on the shape. You can make a variety of smiles by varying the size, color, and shape of the teeth, lips, and skin. This is a good opportunity to highlight the diversity among us.

3. Cover the decorated smile shapes with clear Con-Tact paper.

4. Glue each smile shape onto a tongue depressor.

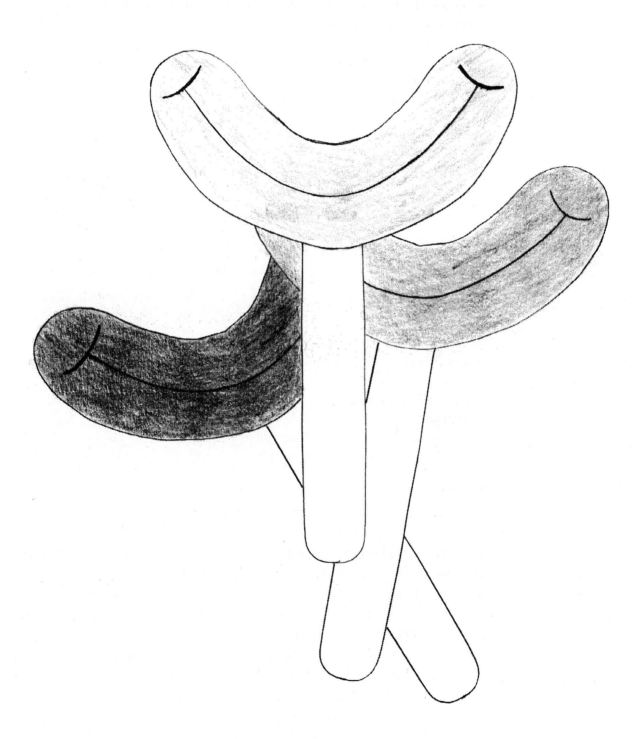

ATTENTION
GRABBER

Stuffed Animal Wand

Special Needs

Toddler

Transition Strategy

Those little stuffed animals that talk, sing, or play music when you push the hidden button in the stomach (or squeeze the paw) are very intriguing to children. Make use of this by turning such a stuffed animal into a wand. Find a small stuffed animal and insert a dowel into it, and you have a wand that required very little time or work to prepare. Pull out the wand while you are waiting in line or for the bus, or use it to grab children's attention at the start of group time. Tell the children you have a special animal that wants to come to group today. Pick children who are ready to listen to push the button.

These wonderful wands stimulate various senses, which makes them very appropriate for toddlers. The wands can also be made with small stuffed animals that don't have a built-in music or talking button. Use a plain stuffed animal for the wand and talk to the children about special things happening in your classroom, such as a special visitor. Use an animal that matches your topic (a dolphin if you are talking about a trip to the zoo or a squirrel if you are talking about signs of fall). Look for small stuffed animals at garage sales or ask parents to donate animals their children are no longer interested in. Discount stores also carry seasonal or theme animals on clearance sales at the end of a season.

Materials

Small stuffed animal with built-in music or talking button
9-inch dowel (⅜–½ inch wide)
Craft glue
Utility knife or scissors
Sandpaper
Optional: Colored plastic or electrician's tape
          1 yard of narrow satin ribbon

Directions

1. Sand one end of the dowel smooth, unless you are planning to wrap it with electrician's tape. This will be the wand's handle.

2. Cut a small slit in the center of the bottom of the stuffed animal with the utility knife or scissors.

3. Put glue on the non-sanded end of the dowel. Insert into the slit in the stuffed animal. Put a small amount of glue around the slit in the animal to prevent further tearing.

4. Optional: Wrap the dowel with the plastic or electrician's tape to make a nicer looking stick. If you do this, you can skip step 1.

5. Optional: Tie ribbon in a pretty bow and glue it to the base of wand.

STRETCHER

Sponge Balls

Transition Strategy

Create an eye-catching, colorful pom-pom ball using an array of brightly colored sponges. Use the sponge pom-pom balls at group time when the kids need a little stretching time. When sitting in a circle, throw the balls to each other, calling out names before throwing. Throw two or three balls into the circle and challenge the children to keep all the balls going at one time. Children can also use these balls alone by hanging onto the rubber band and using them like mini punching balls. The bright colors and soft feel of these balls will be especially appealing to toddlers and children with attention difficulties. Note: Teacher supervision is necessary when using sponge pom-pom balls with toddlers, because they may be able to bite off pieces of the sponge.

Variations

★ **Settler:** Use sponge pom-pom balls as a sensory soother to settle children.

★ **Attention Grabber:** Sponge pom-pom balls can be used the way you use bean-bags. Toss them to the children and say their names as an attention grabber at group time or as an excuser to transition them to another activity.

Materials

Foam-type sponges in six different colors, approximately 6 by 4 by 1 inch (three sponges per ball)

Two large heavy-duty rubber bands (14 inches around) per ball

Directions

1. Cut each sponge lengthwise into either 4, 8, or 16 strips (see illustration).

2. If sponge is cut into fourths, gather two strips of each of the six colors into a bunch. If sponge is cut into 8 strips, gather 4 pieces of each color together. If cut into 16 strips, gather 8 pieces of each color together.

3. Wrap one of the rubber bands three to four times around the center of the sponge pieces until they are held securely together. Wrap the second rubber band one time around the first. Loop one end through the other and pull securely down to create a handle out of the rubber band.

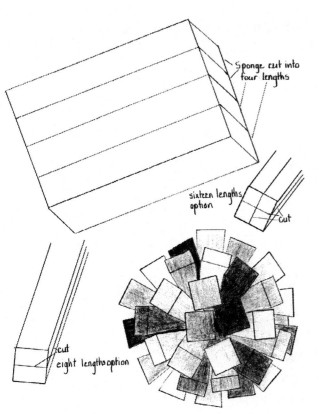

Sponge cut into four lengths

sixteen lengths option

cut

cut

eight lengths option

STRETCHER

Tube Roller

Transition Strategy

One of a toddler's favorite activities is to pull things around a room. These Tube Rollers allow a toddler to do that, and they are very easy, inexpensive, and quick to make. A Tube Roller is simply two heavy-duty cardboard tubes strung together with a circle of cording. Toddlers can hold onto the cording and pull the tubes behind them. Keep a basket of Tube Rollers handy for times when your toddlers need to stretch those muscles but you don't want to get toys off the shelf.

Materials

Two heavy-duty cardboard tubes, each 12–18 inches long, one slightly smaller in diameter than the other (available through Discount School Supplies—see appendix B—or from carpet suppliers)

Cotton cording, ⅜–½ inch wide and 1 yard long (available in fabric stores)

Optional: Permanent markers or stickers

Directions

1.   Thread cording through the two cardboard tubes. Knot ends of the cording together.

2.   Optional: Decorate tubes with permanent marker or stickers to stimulate the sense of sight.

3.   For easy storage, place one tube inside the other.

STRETCHER
Mirroring

Transition Strategy

For a quick and easy stretcher that requires no preparation, try Mirroring. You can either have the children mirror your actions or pair up older preschoolers to mirror each other. Talk to the children about looking at themselves in a mirror. Explain that what they see in the mirror is an exact copy of what they are doing. Move your arms and legs in slow motion and have the children pretend they are your mirrors by moving exactly the same way as you do:

* Move your hands and arms in a circular motion, opposite of each other, in front of your body.
* Raise your legs one at a time and slowly kick out in front of you.
* Bend at the waist—forward, backward, and to the sides.
* Nod your head.
* Stretch your arms way up high, out from your sides, and then down to your toes.

Another option is to move just your mouth in different ways and have children mirror your mouth movements. When you first introduce this activity, it might be easier for you to mirror a child's movements, to help the children understand the concept of mirroring. After they have a handle on this stretcher, one of the children could be the leader. Remember to position yourself with the group of children so you can be a good model of how to mirror the leader.

Variation

* **Routine Change:** Because Mirroring can be done without any props, it makes an excellent strategy to use during routine changes such as getting ready for outdoor play. While some children are waiting for the rest of the group to finish dressing, engage in some facial or body movements for mirroring.

STRETCHER

Streamers on a Hoop

Toddler

Transition Strategy

When it's time to get up and do some stretching, there are few things children love more than singing and dancing, especially if they have something pretty to dance with. This inexpensive and easy-to-make prop is colorful and makes a nice noise when the children are dancing. The children are sure to ask for Streamers on a Hoop over and over again.

Streamers on a Hoop are made with margarine-tub lids and garbage bags. You can make enough for every child to hold several. And if they break, it costs almost nothing to replace them. Streamers on a Hoop are particularly safe for toddlers because they are round and have no sharp edges to poke soft bodies.

Variation

★ Streamers on a Hoop can also be made with shower curtain hoops and cloth ribbons. It's a great way to use those old shower curtain hoops. Tie colorful pieces of narrow ribbon onto the hoop. Look for spools of ribbon in the craft section of discount stores. These hoops are a little more costly to make but are also more durable.

Materials

Plastic margarine-tub lids
Colored plastic garbage bags,
    or plastic surveyor's tape,
    ¾–1 inch wide

Directions

1.   Cut the inside out of a margarine-tub lid, leaving approximately ½–¾ inch for an edge.

2.   Cut the garbage bags (or surveyor's tape) into strips about 1 inch wide and 24–48 inches long.

3.   Fold the strips lengthwise and tie onto the ring, knotting them in place.

STRETCHER

Balloon on a Ring

Transition Strategy

Children love balloons—particularly the Mylar polyester-film balloons available in grocery stores and floral shops. Having the chance to hold the balloon for one verse of a song will prompt even the shyest dancer to emerge from your group. Have the children stand or sit in a circle. To the tune of "Where Is Thumbkin," sing the following song:

> Dance around, dance around, dance around, I sing
> Put your hands behind your back and I'll give you the ring.

When it's a child's turn to hold the Balloon on a Ring, she moves around the circle and picks another child to hold onto the ring. Children can be encouraged to move around the circle in a variety of ways, such as tiptoeing, hopping, or skipping.

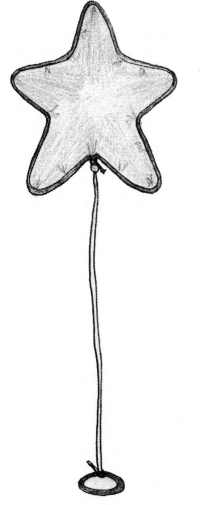

Note: Avoid using latex balloons. Some children are allergic to them. Also, when they break, you have small pieces of rubber that toddlers may put in their mouths, swallow, and choke on.

Variation

* **Magical Moment:** For a Magical Moment on a field trip, take a helium-filled balloon along. It's easy for children to spot you and know where to gather.

Materials

Mylar balloon (helium filled) with string or ribbon attached
Shower-curtain ring

Directions

Tie the balloon onto the shower-curtain ring.

Shape-Up Aerobics

Transition Strategy

Tips for how to exercise are everywhere these days—in magazines, in newspapers, and on TV. Doing aerobics with the kids will make them feel just like mom, dad, or big brother or sister, and it will help them get the wiggles out. These picture props, which show the kids how to move, are simple and fast to make. Each card has a stick figure in a different body position and movement, such a bending at the waist or hopping on one foot. Keep the cards by your group area to have on hand whenever a little exercise is needed. Have a child pick a card from the can; do the action on the card together.

Materials

Unruled white 5-by-7-inch index cards
Tin can for storage
Markers

Directions

Using the illustrations below as a guide, draw one stick figure per card illustrating the following movements: doing jumping jacks, stretching arms and legs out, twirling arms, bending knees, marching, hopping on one foot, running, touching toes, and tapping knees.

EXTENDER ## "Toddlers Like To" Book

Transition Strategy

Children, especially toddlers, love to look at pictures of themselves. The pages of this homemade photo book are easily replaceable at little cost, just in case they get damaged through everyday wear and tear. When one teacher is finishing up the diapering or getting lunch on the table, the other teacher can sit down with the other children to look at the "Toddlers Like To" Book. Pictures can easily be changed to spark new interest. These books are inexpensive to make, so you can easily make a book for each toddler in your room.

Variations

★ **Magic Carpet Activity:** When you're making your book, include a photo of each toddler in your room. As a child comes over for "drop and flop" time with you, flip to that child's picture in the book and sing this song to the tune "Where is Thumbkin?":

> Where is (child's name), where is (child's name)?
> Please stand up, please stand up.
> Turn yourself around, give yourself a hug.
> Then sit down, please sit down.

Beware—the other toddlers may come running to be a part of this fun activity.

★ **Magical Moment:** Stick several of these little books in your backpack or bag and pull them out to look at if you have to spend time waiting.

Materials

Small photo-album refill pages
File folders or poster board
2 metal rings (1-inch diameter)
Photos of children doing a variety
   of activities throughout the day
Double-sided sticking tape

Directions

1. Cut file folders or poster board to fit inside the photo pages. Save two pages to be the covers.

2. On the cover page write the words "Toddlers Like To . . ."

3. Tape photos onto the poster board with double-sided sticking tape. On the poster board below each photo, write words describing what the child is doing in the picture. Slip inside the photo page.

4. Attach the pages together with the metal rings, placing the photo pages between the front and back covers.

Move-Your-Body Cube

Transition Strategy

These body-parts cubes made with looped Velcro fabric are soft and squishy and very appealing to children, particularly toddlers and children with sensory-integration difficulties (see Glossary). When you have a short amount of time to fill, use a combination of these cubes to get the children moving. On one cube attach pictures of different parts of the body that move. On another cube attach numbers made of stiffened felt. Have the children stand in a circle. Taking turns, have a child throw the body-parts cube and then the cube with numbers. The child then moves the body part that was rolled in any way he desires, the number of times that was thrown on the numbers cube (for example, bend an elbow six times, or nod your head five times). Make sure there is enough time for every child in the circle to have a turn throwing a cube.

Variations

* **Extender:** Exchange the numerals with circles made from stiffened felt in six different colors. Another way to extend group time is to roll the cube and tell the children who are wearing that color to stand up. Roll the color cube again. Children wearing that color can stand up and the rest sit down.

* **Extender:** Place geometric shapes on the cube and roll it. Have children name an object in the room that has that shape.

* **Excuser:** Attach only the numbers that represent the ages of your children to the cube. When it's time to excuse them from group time, roll the cube. Children the age of whatever number comes up may leave and move on to the next activity.

Materials

Two cubes made of looped Velcro fabric (see appendix F)
File folders or body-shaped decorative notepads
Clear Con-Tact paper
Water-base markers
Small pieces of adhesive-backed Velcro
Stiffened felt or heavy interfacing material
Number stencils (3 inches)

Directions

Body Parts Pictures

1. Purchase body-shaped decorative notepads, or cut file folders into the shape of a body.

2. Label a different body part on each of the six body shapes.

3. Cover the paper shapes with clear Con-Tact paper.

4. Attach 2 small pieces of Velcro onto the back of each body shape.

5. Stick the pictures onto one of the fabric cubes, one body shape per side.

Stiffened Felt Numbers

1. Trace and cut out numbers 1 through 6 from stiffened felt.

2. Attach small pieces of Velcro onto the backs of the numbers.

3. Stick the numbers onto the other looped Velcro fabric cube, one number per side.

Color Cards

Special Needs
Toddler

Transition Strategy

Activities that extend your time do not need to be complicated and involve lots of preparation. Color Cards are simply strips of different-colored file folders kept on a ring for handy use. They are made small enough to slide in and out of your pocket. When you have a few minutes to wait till the next activity is ready, pull out the cards. Show the children one color at a time and have them find something in the room that is that color or think of something that is that color. Having an example to look at while you say the name of the color is a great help for toddlers who are just learning their colors. Some file folders come with bright colors on one side and a pastel tint of the same color on the other side. Use these to double the use of the color cards.

Variations

* **Magical Moment:** Take your Color Cards with you on a field trip for a Magical Moment activity. Sing this song to the tune "Row, Row, Row Your Boat":

  Colors of the rainbow
  Red and blue and green
  Yellow, orange, and purple
  Which one do you see?

  Hold up one color and have the children name it.

* **Excuser:** As the bus arrives to pick up the children, excuse them by holding up a Color Card and having every child wearing a coat of that color leave the group.

Materials

File folders in 6 different colors
Clear Con-Tact paper
Paper punch (a shape such as a star or heart is a fun variation)
1 metal ring (1-inch diameter)

Directions

1. Cut file folders into 1-by-6-inch strips.

2. Cover the file folder pieces with Con-Tact paper.

3. Punch a hole in one end of each of the strips in the same spot.

4. Put all the strips together on the metal ring.

EXTENDER

Where Is the Animal?

Transition Strategy

This game is a great way to help your children sharpen their listening skills. All you need is a variety of stuffed animals that make noises when you push the button in the stomach. While the children in your group have their eyes closed, have one child pick one stuffed animal out of a basket and hide with it somewhere in your classroom or just outside in the hall (if that is appropriate). Sing the following phrase to the tune of "Where is Thumbkin," naming the child who is hiding: "Where is Billy, where is Billy?" The child answers from the hiding spot by singing, "Here I am, here I am." When he answers, he pushes the button of the animal he is holding to make its noise. The other children have to guess where the hidden child is, without getting up and moving around in the room. Continue the song by singing, "Where was Billy hiding? Where was Billy hiding?" Now finish the song by singing, "Please come back, please come back." At this point, Billy can reveal himself and return to the group.

Variation

* If you have enough "talking" animals for each child to have one, try this version. Give each child in your small group an animal and have her hide someplace in the room. You start by singing about one animal, such as "Where is the puppy? Where is the puppy?" The child with the puppy pushes the button to make the animal sound. Then sing, "How are you today, puppy?" The child pushes the button again. Conclude by singing, "Please come back, please come back." That child returns. Let her choose the animal to sing for next and then join in singing. Repeat until all animals have been found.

* **Extender:** Put several animals in a large "feely box." Choose a child to reach in and push the sound button of an animal. All the children guess what animal makes that sound. Have the child pull the animal out and see if they were right. For added fun, push the button one more time and have all the children make the sound with the animal. Repeat until the next activity is ready to begin.

Emotions Song

Transition Strategy

This is a great extender because it requires no props or preparation and can be done wherever you are, either in the classroom or out. Simply pick one of your favorite songs and sing it with the children. Afterwards, talk to the children about how someone sounds when she is sad, tired, angry, and so on. Say, "How do you suppose someone who is sad would sing that song?" Now sing the same song with the children as though you are all sad, then scared, shy, angry, and so on. Pick any emotion you can pretend to be. Be sure the children understand that this is pretend. Young children, particularly toddlers and children with disabilities, rely on you to be a stable, calm person for them at all times. They will not understand your acting angry or sad if you do not tell them it is just that—acting.

Variation

*   For an optional addition to this activity, make a puppet on a stick that displays the emotion you are trying to portray through singing. Hold it up while singing the song.

Materials

File folders
Markers
Tongue depressors
Glue

Directions

1. Draw a 3- to 4-inch circle on a file folder. Cut it out.

2. Draw a face on the circle depicting the emotion you want to portray.

3. Glue the circle onto a tongue depressor.

Scrubber Puzzles

Transition Strategy

For a puzzle with a different feel to it, try making some of these Scrubber Puzzles. These simple little matching puzzles are made from white kitchen scrubbers that clean pots and pans. By cutting a scrubber in half and putting matching objects on both sides of the scrubber, you can make a quick and interesting puzzle. These scrubbers can be drawn on with permanent markers to match the various abilities of the children in your class. For preschoolers, make a set of puzzles with numerals on one side and the same number of objects or shapes on the other side to count. For toddlers, draw large colored dots on each side of the puzzle to match colors.

Variation

* **Extender:** Have children sit in a circle. Give each child one half of a puzzle. Lay the other halves of the puzzles in the middle of the circle. Choose one child at a time to come forward and get the other half of his puzzle. He returns to his place and puts the puzzle together in front of him.

Materials

White kitchen scrubbers
Permanent markers
Self-sealing plastic bags

Directions

1. Cut each scrubber in half. To add variety, make the cut a zigzag or a wavy line.

2. Use permanent markers to draw matching objects (either numbers or colors as described above) on both sides of the puzzles (see illustration).

3. Store in self-sealing plastic bags.

3-D Snow-Person

Transition Strategy

Few things in your classroom will be as popular as this cute little stuffed snow-person. The children will be able to dress and redress it as often as they wish. Using real scarves, hats, and mittens to dress the snow-person almost makes it come alive in the classroom. All parts of its face and body come apart so that children can reassemble the snow-person however they want. Watch the children get silly and stick arms to the face and eyeballs to the bottom. Be sure to give the children enough time to play with it in an extended Magic Carpet time.

Materials

White Velcro looped fabric
Polyester stuffing
Black and orange felt
Pieces of white Velcro
Assorted winter scarves
Assorted small hats (straw, stocking, etc.)
Fabric glue or hot-glue gun
Sewing machine
Optional: Large box
       Light blue Con-Tact paper
       White Con-Tact paper
       Stencil-cutting machine

Directions

Snow-Person

1. Cut three rectangles of white looped Velcro fabric in the following sizes: one 17-by-34-inch rectangle; one 15-by-28-inch rectangle; one 13-by-22-inch rectangle. See figure 1.

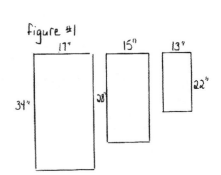

figure #1

2. Machine sew the three rectangles, right sides together, into three tube shapes (along the 17-inch, 15-inch, and 13-inch sides). See figure 2.

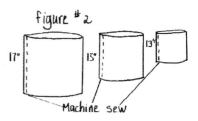

figure #2

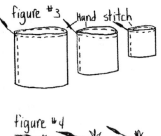

figure #3 Hand stitch

3. Hand stitch around one open end (about 1 inch in) of each of the tubes. See figure 3.

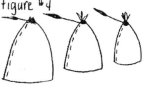

figure #4

4. Pull the thread taut, gathering up the opening, and twist the thread around the gathered fabric a couple of times; tie off. Do this on all three tubes. See figure 4.

figure #5

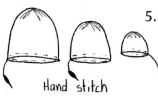

Hand stitch

5. Turn the tubes right side out and hand stitch around the other end. See figure 5.

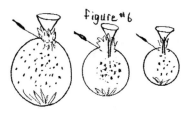

figure #6

6. Pull the thread taut, gathering up the opening until it is almost completely shut. Fill with polyester stuffing. See figure 6.

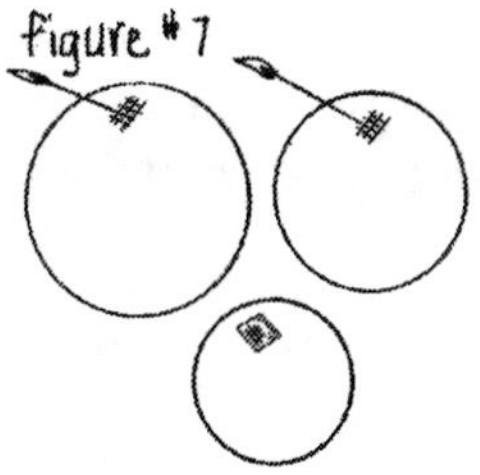

figure #7

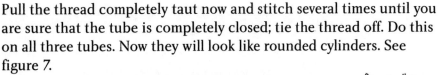

7. Pull the thread completely taut now and stitch several times until you are sure that the tube is completely closed; tie the thread off. Do this on all three tubes. Now they will look like rounded cylinders. See figure 7.

figure #8

8. Glue a long piece of Velcro to both gathered ends of the medium-size ball. Now your snowballs are done, and they should stick together when placed on top of each other. See figure 8.

9. Cut a triangular shape out of orange felt, all three sides about 4 inches long, for the carrot nose. Also cut a circle 1½ inches in diameter. See figure 9. Machine sew two sides of the triangle together and turn. See figure 10. Stuff the carrot shape with polyester stuffing and hand sew the circle on the open end. See figure 11.

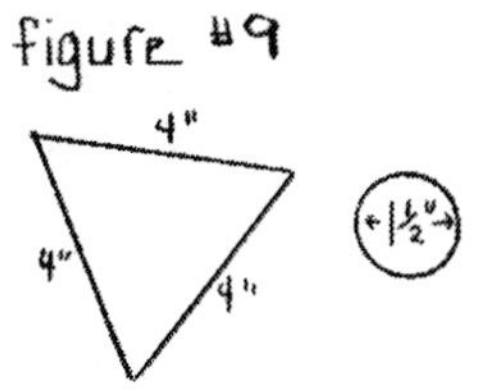

figure #9

4"

4"   4"

←1½"→

figure #10

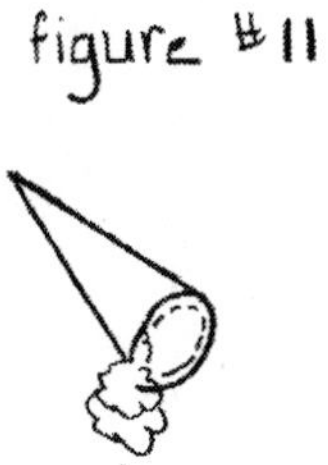

figure #11

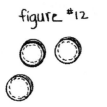

figure #12

10. Cut six 1½-inch-diameter circles out of the orange felt to make the buttons. Put a very small amount of polyester stuffing between two of the circles and machine sew around the edge of the circle. Do this for each of the three buttons. See figure 12.

11. Cut four 1½-inch-diameter circles out of the black felt to make the eyes. Repeat the same process as with the buttons.

12. Cut eight ¾-inch squares out of the black felt for coal pieces for the mouth. Machine stitch two squares together around the edges. Repeat until you have four pieces of coal for the mouth. See figure 13.

figure # 13

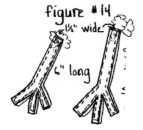

figure #14
1½" wide
6" long

13. Cut four branch shapes for the arms and hands from black felt. They should be about 1½ inches wide at the base and about 6 inches long. Machine sew around the edges of the branch, leaving the base open. Stuff the arms/hands with polyester stuffing and then sew the base closed. See figure 14.

14. Glue a small piece of Velcro on the back or end of each facial feature, button, and arm with a hot-glue gun. These are now ready to be attached and reattached to the snow-person.

Storage Box

1. Cover the box with blue Con-Tact paper.

2. Cut snowflakes out of white Con-Tact paper using a stencil-cutting machine or your own snowflake pattern. Decorate the outside of the box with the snowflakes.

3. Place all pieces of the snow-person, as well as assorted scarves and hats, in the box for easy storage.

Water Pillows

Transition Strategy

Infants and young toddlers will love these pillows made of clear heavy-duty plastic and filled with colorful objects to watch. Just set infants on the floor next to the pillow and let them push and tap on the pillow to make everything flow gently around.

Variation

★ Water Pillows can also be made with two-gallon self-sealing plastic freezer bags. Because they are made of lighter-weight plastic, they will wear out more quickly. Slip another two-gallon bag over the water-filled bag, remove air, and tape for added strength.

Materials

Plastic "flow" (a tube of heavyweight plastic approximately six inches wide and two feet long, with handles on the ends—available from Discount School Supplies—see appendix B)

Assortment of tiny colorful beads, erasers, small Koosh balls, plastic sequins, or any other small objects that can withstand the water and do not have sharp edges

Duct tape

Water

Directions

1. Fill the plastic flow halfway with water.

2. Place assortment of objects into the water.

3. Gently push on bag to remove excess air, close, and seal the bag with duct tape.

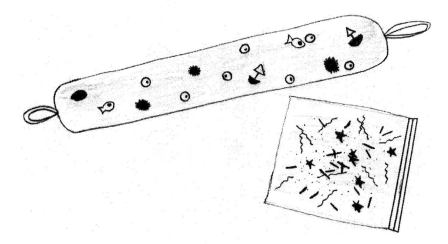

Folder of Flowers

Transition Strategy

File folder games make wonderful Magic Carpet activities because they are inexpensive, so you can make many of them. You will want to make several Folder of Flowers games because they are so appealing to children. They will all want to touch the colorful flowers and play with the three-dimensional bees and butterflies. This game is particularly nice because it is so versatile—you can decide how to play the game depending on the developmental level of the children you work with. Preschoolers can move the bees and butterflies around; as they get older, they can count or sort the pieces or match colors. With the same goals in mind, be creative and use other objects such as birds and eggs in nests or frogs and ducks on lily pads. Try transportation stickers on a land, sea, or air folder.

Materials

1 colored file folder
Red, green, yellow, and
    blue looped Velcro
    fabric (approximately
    ⅛ yard of each)
Spray adhesive (3M
    Super 77 works well)
Optional: stencil-cutting
    machine
Self-sealing plastic bag
Chenille bees (available
    from Oriental Trading—see appendix B)
Small craft butterflies (available from craft stores)
Tiny pieces of adhesive-backed Velcro

Directions

1. On the front of the file folder write the words "Bees & Butterflies."

2. Cut several flowers with removable centers out of the red, yellow, and blue looped Velcro fabric using a stencil-cutting machine (see illustration). If you don't have access to a stencil-cutting machine, cut your own flowers and removable centers.

3. Draw and cut out stems and leaves by hand.

4. Arrange flowers on the inside of the file folder, exchanging the colors of the centers of the flowers, so that each flower has a center of a different color.

5. Attach the flowers, centers, stems, and leaves to the file folder with spray adhesive.

6. For storage of the bees and butterflies, tape the sides and bottom of the plastic bag onto the back of the file folder (see illustration).

7. Attach a tiny piece of the adhesive-backed Velcro onto each of the bees and butterflies. Store in the plastic bag.

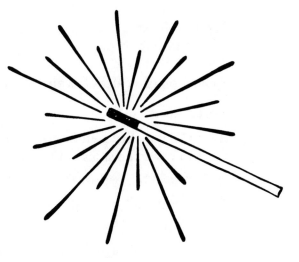

Box-o-Books

Transition Strategy

If you collect sets of children's books and the trinkets that go with them, then this is a terrific way for you to use the books with the children. The Box-o-Books is a small decorated box filled with small books and objects that go with the books. For example, an Eric Carle box is decorated with pages of an Eric Carle calendar and filled with Eric Carle books (board books are perfect for toddlers), such as *The Very Hungry Caterpillar,* and coordinating toys—anything caterpillar- and food-related. An Ellen Stowel Walsh box is filled with her books about mice along with several little homemade stuffed mice. The box is decorated with the pictures taken from a second copy of the book. Place the box on your Magic Carpet shelf and let the children enjoy it, as they will. Or gather your Box-o-Books and invite a toddler to come with you for a "drop and flop" time. Let her manipulate the trinkets as you read the book.

Materials

Small durable boxes with covers, large enough to hold the collections of
    books and trinkets
Calendar pages, or second copy of one of the books
Spray adhesive
Clear Con-Tact paper
Colored duct tape
Collection of small books and related objects

Directions

1.   Cut out the calendar pages or pages from the second copy of one book to cover the sides of the box.

2.   Attach the pictures to the outside of the box with spray adhesive.

3.   Cover each side with clear Con-Tact paper.

4.   Reinforce edges with colorful duct tape.

5.   Fill the box with the books and related objects.

Mini Sound Shakers

Transition Strategy

These sound jars make good use out of all those 35mm film canisters in your storage closet. Children will enjoy shaking them to find the pair with the matching sounds. It's a great activity to sharpen those little ears. The jars are small and easily cleaned, so they make a nice choice of materials for your Magic Carpet shelf. For every matching pair of sound jars, draw matching colored dots or use matching colored sticky dots on the bottom of the jar. Children can check the dots to see if they made a correct match.

Variations

* **Stretcher:** Use the sound jars as shakers for a stretching activity. Give each child a jar to shake as they move to music.

* **Excuser:** Give each child one sound jar; you take the matching jars. Shake one jar, then have children take turns shaking theirs. If the sound matches yours, the child returns his jar to you and leaves group for the next activity.

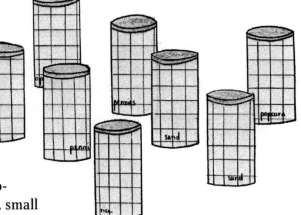

Materials

Plastic 35mm film
    canisters
Colored Con-Tact
    paper
Quick-bond glue
Assorted filler material
    such as rice, sand, salt, pop-
    corn, dried beans, pennies, small
    erasers, etc.
Permanent markers in assorted colors
Small box or bag for storage

Directions

1. Fill pairs of canisters with identical filler materials, filling each canister no more than half full so there is room for the material to move around inside and make a noise.

2. Glue the lid onto each canister with quick-bond glue.

3. Cover the canister with colored Con-Tact paper to add eye appeal.

4. With permanent markers, draw large colored dots on the bottoms of the canisters indicating matching sets, or use matching colored sticky dots.

Teacher Pockets

Special Needs

Toddler

Transition Strategy

You can turn a simple carpenter's apron into a fun and versatile teaching tool in no time flat! Simply stitch squares of looped Velcro fabric to the fronts of the apron pockets. Fill the pockets with sensory materials that have pieces of Velcro attached to the backs. Use materials such as rough sandpaper, glossy wrapping paper, or a small bumpy gourd or walnut. At waiting times, pull the materials out of the pockets one at a time, stick them to the front of the apron, and talk about how each one feels. Give the children turns to pick items out of your pockets to attach to the apron.

Variation

★ **Extender:** Use the carpenter's apron as an extender at group time when lunch or snack isn't quite ready, the bus hasn't arrived, or the next activity is still being set up.

Materials

Carpenter's apron (available in lumber and hardware stores)

Looped Velcro fabric (approximately 8 by 18 inches)

Small pieces of sensory materials (sandpaper, wrapping paper, nuts, paper with glue dried on, satin, velvet, bubble packing sheets, lamb's wool)

Small pieces of Velcro

Spray adhesive

Poster board or old file folders

Directions

1. Cut the looped Velcro fabric into rectangular pieces that will fit onto the fronts of the apron pockets.

2. Glue (or hand sew) a piece onto the front of each apron pocket with spray adhesive. Before gluing, place old newspaper or scrap paper inside the pocket to prevent any glue from seeping through the apron material.

3. For added strength, attach the sensory material onto a piece of poster-board or file folder. Cut the sensory materials into pieces that will fit easily into the apron pockets. Attach small piece of Velcro onto the back of each sensory material with either the sticky backing or a small amount of craft glue.

See-Through Crayons

Transition Strategy

Focus on the children's sense of sight with these crayon-shaped cellophane cards, and help them learn colors at the same time. When you look through a card, the whole world turns the color of the card. They are sturdy enough to give to toddlers to use on their own. Have them available for children to use while getting dressed to go outside or while waiting to get diapers changed; set them on high chairs for older infants. They love to sit and just look through the cards.

Materials

Heavy poster board
Colored vinyl page protectors—red, blue, yellow
Colored Con-Tact paper—red, blue, yellow
Tape
Colored plastic tape—red, blue, yellow
Optional: Stencil-cutting machine with crayon-shaped stencil

Directions

1. For each "crayon," cut two 8-by-5-inch rectangles out of poster board.

2. Cover with colored Con-Tact paper.

3. Draw a crayon shape in the center of each rectangle and cut it out, or use a stencil-cutting machine to cut the shape out. Discard the cut-out middle and keep the frame.

4. For each card, cut two or three pieces of vinyl page protector into 7-by-4-inch rectangles. Make them one color (multiple layers give extra strength), or put two vinyl sheets of different primary colors together to create a secondary color. Place the layers together between the two poster-board frame pieces and tape into place.

5. Tape around the outside edges of the poster board with the colored plastic tape.

Musical Pictures

Transition Strategy

Children are always curious about something they can feel. They will be drawn to this picture of a giant clown face on the wall, and when they come close they will see a large felt nose to push. Won't they be surprised when they touch it and it plays music! Place the clown face anywhere children have to wait in a group, such as outside a bathroom, in a hall where they wait for the bus, or by the door to the playground. Add a piece of a colorful, curly wig and a ruffly collar made from netting for more textures to feel. A second option for a musical picture is to draw a large fish bowl on poster board. Glue music discs randomly in the water area and cover them with felt fish. A third option is to draw a garden of large flowers. Place a different music disc in the center of each flower and cover with felt centers.

Materials

Poster board (full-size
    sheet)
Water-base markers
Clear Con-Tact paper
Push-button music
    disc (available in
    craft stores)
Felt (approximately 3-
    inch circle)
Craft glue
Optional: colorful,
    curly wig and ruffly
    clown collar

Directions

1. Draw a large
    clown face on the poster board (see illustration).

2. Cover with clear Con-Tact paper.

3. Glue the push-button music disc in the nose spot.

4. Run a line of glue around the edge of the felt circle, then press down around the disc, covering it.

MAGICAL MOMENT

Bubbles on the Go

Special Needs

Toddler

Transition Strategy

Children of all ages love bubbles. Bubbles create a fun, magical time for the children (and staff), especially on the playground, at the park, or on a field trip. When it's time to gather children together or while waiting for a bus, pull out your bubbles and you are guaranteed to have every child's attention in a snap! Be on the lookout for a bubble dispenser that hangs around your neck on a rope. A variety of discount stores carry these now, particularly at holiday times and in the spring and summer. Oriental Trading Company (address in appendix B) sells a wide variety of bubble necklaces. Or carry a small bottle of bubbles in your backpack.

MAGICAL
MOMENT

Mini Microphone

Special Needs

Toddler

Transition Strategy

This Mini Microphone is fast and easy to make, and it's great when you have to "take your show on the road." Stick this little "microphone" in your pocket, and when you're on a field trip or visiting the library, pull it out to make announcements to the children. Whisper, since this is a "mini" microphone, and the children will magically quiet down to listen carefully.

Materials

New small spongy-ball cat toy
Pencil with eraser top
Glue

Directions

1. Break about ⅓ off the lead end of the pencil (or find a used pencil about ⅔ the length of a new pencil).

2. Make a small slit in the spongy ball. Put a small amount of glue on the broken end of the pencil and insert it in the hole of the ball.

    Note: The eraser of the pencil provides a soft, safe end for toddlers to hold.

EXCUSER

Count the Steps

Transition Strategy

This is a simple strategy for an older group of preschoolers, and it requires no advance preparation. As you move from one area to the next between activities, have the children count their steps. Children can do this individually and compare the number of steps it took each of them to get to their destination. Or, for longer distances, walk along with the children and count your steps together. This is a wonderful way to help children learn to count to larger numbers. For children who are easily distracted as they move around the room, having the counting to concentrate on while they move will be a big help. For a simple variation, when you excuse children from the group, give directions in each child's ear using different voices, from a whisper to a giant's deep voice. Or instruct them to move in different ways, such as tiny baby steps or giant steps, and to count their steps as they go. It will be fun to compare the numbers at their destination.

Variations

* **Routine Change:** For routine changes that require moving children from one room to another, attach shoe prints with clear Con-Tact paper to the floor from the classroom door to a frequent destination such as the bathroom, cubbies, or lunchroom. Following the path will slow the children down, promote concentration, and keep this transition orderly.

* **Routine Change:** During routine changes, encourage children to engage in imaginary play as they move through the hall. They can pretend to be dinosaurs looking for food or walking through mud, or eagles soaring.

Twirling Ribbon Wand

Special Needs

Toddler

Transition Strategy

This beautiful wand will transfix children as they wait to be excused from group. Made with ribbons of many different colors, it creates a swirling rainbow for the children to watch. Just twirl the wand between your fingers as you move around the group of children. Recite the following poem as you move:

Bibbity bobbity boo
Go to the small-group table
When the wand stops at you!

Variations

★ **Settler:** Use this colorful wand to magically settle children by waving it over the group.

★ **Attention Grabber:** Grab children's attention by pointing the wand to an object, a box, or a basket strategically placed in the center of the group-time area.

★ **Stretcher:** Give a Twirling Ribbon Wand to each child when the group needs a stretch.

★ **Extender:** Pass the wand from child to child to create a "colorful" story. The teacher starts by choosing one ribbon and begins the story using that color in the first sentence. For example:

Teacher: One bright summer morning Lucy woke up and looked out the window at the beautiful blue sky (hold up blue ribbon).

First child: She saw a robin with a red breast (hold up red ribbon) flying through the air.

Second child: Soon the robin flew down to the green grass (hold up green ribbon).

And so on... Continue until the next activity is ready to begin.

Materials

Narrow satin ribbon (¼ inch or ⅛ inch) in a variety of colors
¼-inch dowel, 9 inches long, or colorful pencil

Plastic tape or electrician's tape
Sandpaper

Directions

1. Sand one end of the dowel smooth, unless you plan to cover the entire dowel with electrical tape or use a pencil.

2. Cut the desired number of ribbons into lengths of 6–8 inches (can be the same or varying lengths).

3. Gather ribbons into a bunch on one end. Tape securely onto the end of the dowel, making sure you catch each piece of ribbon under the tape.

4. Continue taping the length of the dowel with the plastic tape.

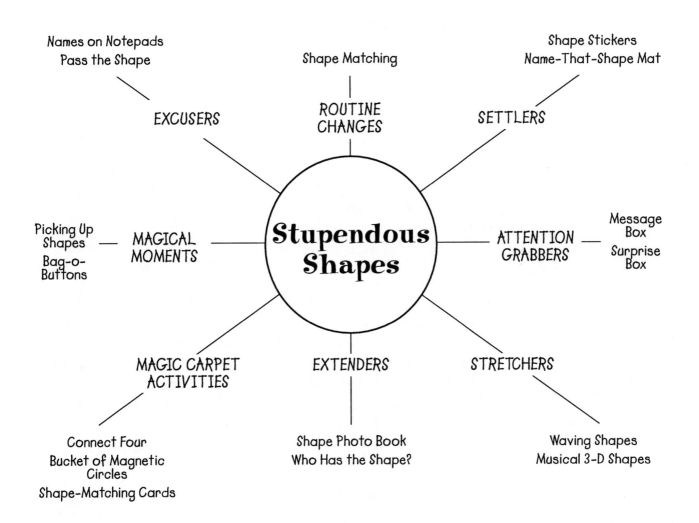

Names on Notepads
Pass the Shape

Shape Matching

Shape Stickers
Name-That-Shape Mat

EXCUSERS

ROUTINE
CHANGES

SETTLERS

Picking Up
Shapes
Bag-o-
Buttons

MAGICAL
MOMENTS

**Stupendous
Shapes**

ATTENTION
GRABBERS

Message
Box
Surprise
Box

MAGIC CARPET
ACTIVITIES

EXTENDERS

STRETCHERS

Connect Four
Bucket of Magnetic
Circles
Shape-Matching Cards

Shape Photo Book
Who Has the Shape?

Waving Shapes
Musical 3-D Shapes

Shape Matching

Transition Strategy

This tactic will help the children in your class learn shapes and will provide focus when moving from activity to activity. When each child arrives, he is given a shape necklace made from art foam. Throughout the day he finds a matching shape sit-upon at group time and a matching shape place mat at meal or snack time. These shapes can be made from either colored transparent vinyl or a vinyl tablecloth; both materials appeal to young children's senses. Children can be given either the same shape for a number of days or a different shape each day. Use the same shape for several days in a row for toddlers and children with attention difficulties, because change is more difficult for them.

Materials

Art-foam sheets (available in craft stores or in the craft section of discount stores), enough sheets to cut one 3-to-4-inch shape per child
Vinyl lace (also available in craft stores), 12–15 inches per child
Colored transparent vinyl (available in fabric stores) or a vinyl tablecloth, 12 by 18 inches per child
Paper punch

Directions

Shape Necklace

1. Cut 3-to-4-inch geometric shapes (circle, square, triangle, rectangle, diamond, oval, cross, heart) from art foam, enough for each child to have one shape. You may repeat shapes if you have a large group, or make the same shapes out of different colors (for example, blue, green, and pink circles, triangles, and squares).

2. Punch a hole near the edge of the shape, but far enough in to prevent the edge from tearing.

3. String a piece of vinyl lace through the hole and knot the ends together.

Matching Vinyl Shapes

1. Draw matching shapes using either the colored transparent vinyl or the vinyl tablecloth. They can be any size desired. Note: 12–18 inches is large enough for either a sit-upon or a place mat. Cut out.

SETTLER

Shape Stickers

Special Needs

Toddler

Transition Strategy

For a quick and simple way to help children transition from one activity into the next, try using a sticker. As children move into a new activity, such as group time, place Shape Stickers on the backs of their hands. Placing the sticker on the hand signals to the child that it's time to listen and settle. Settlers are very helpful reminders to those children who have difficulty remembering directions. A reminder about the sticker signal brings a child back on task.

Variation

* **Excuser:** When it's time to excuse children from group time, walk around without saying a word and place a sticker on the hand of each child when it's her turn to leave the group and transition to the next activity.

Name-That-Shape Mat

Transition Strategy

Often prevention is the best method in behavior guidance. Creating a special place for each child to sit at group time will invite her to come to the group area and help her get settled and ready to listen. Brightly colored shapes, made from book-cover material or a vinyl tablecloth, will draw children's attention immediately and pull them into the group area. The children will eagerly find a place to sit. Shapes are placed on the tablecloth to give plenty of space between children, allowing for movement without disagreements about sitting too close or bumping into each other. Preschool children can learn to name the shapes. After they can identify the shapes, you can send children to the mat by having them search for a circle, triangle, or square to sit on.

Materials

One light-colored vinyl tablecloth (large enough for every child in your group to sit on—a 60-inch round or square tablecloth will seat approximately 8–9 children)

Shiny, brightly colored book-cover material, sticky on one side (available in most discount stores)

Optional: Velcro pieces
Clear
Con-Tact
paper

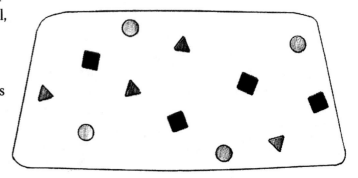

Directions

1. Cut the book cover material into a variety of geometric shapes approximately 8–10 inches across.

2. Place the shapes on the tablecloth, allowing for plenty of space between each shape for children to move. Note: If you use the book-covering material, it might be necessary to place a larger piece of clear Con-Tact paper over the shape to ensure that the shape remains stuck to the tablecloth.

3. Optional: If the tablecloth is placed over a carpet, attach small pieces of the hooked side of Velcro to the corners of the tablecloth to hold it in place.

ATTENTION
GRABBER

Message Box

Transition Strategy

These intriguing little boxes with special messages hidden inside will grab every child's attention and help him transition into the next task at hand. The messages can announce things that are going to happen that day, such as "Today we are going to ___" or "Let's sing a song." Or they can simply say things that make the children feel good, such as "I'm glad you're here today!" To use the Message Box with your group of children, place a few special messages inside the little decorated box and place the box in your seat before the children come to group. When the children arrive at group, create a little mystery surrounding the box by saying, "Oh look what I found on my chair—I wonder what's inside?" Or, if they have seen the box before, say, "I wonder what special message is hidden inside our shape box today?"

Variation

* **Extender:** You can use the Message Box to extend your time together by replacing the messages with short instructions. On the slips of paper, tell the children to look for certain things in the room. Or write the names of their favorite songs and finger plays for the children to sing while waiting for the next activity.

Materials

Small cardboard jewelry box or geometrically shaped box (such as a heart or star)
Decorative Con-Tact paper or white Con-Tact paper
Fine permanent markers
Little slips of paper with messages

Directions

1. Cover a small box with Con-Tact paper. If using white Con-Tact paper, draw geometric shapes on the box (such as squares, circles, rectangles, or hearts).

2. Write messages on slips of paper and place them in the box.

Surprise Box

Special Needs
Toddler

Transition Strategy

This Surprise Box will certainly pique children's curiosity and grab their attention. All you have to do is decorate a box and fill it with things that are the shape you are working on. Place the box in your group area, and when it is time to transition to group time, tell the children to come on over and see what's in the box. They can guess what's in the box, or you can give them clues, or you can slowly pull something out of the box. Have fun with this and create a little mystery around it.

This box is very versatile. You can decorate and fill it with items of any theme. For example, cover the box with white contact paper, decorate it with stickers of musical notes, and fill it with a variety of musical instruments. The possibilities are endless. And when you are done with the unit, you can store all the materials and items used for the unit in the box.

Variation

★ Use a decorative gift bag instead of a box. Gift bags come in a large assortment of designs, and a bag can be found to match any unit or theme, such as a checkerboard bag for a unit on squares, or a bag covered with hearts for a unit on hearts. All you have to do is keep on the lookout for interesting bags.

Materials

Empty cardboard box with a detachable lid (the type used to store files, available in office supply stores, works well)
Con-Tact paper (white or decorative to match your theme)
Props to go with your theme (such as round dishes, old records, or a round wall clock to go with a circle theme)
Optional: Stickers or permanent markers
Decorative gift bag

Directions

1. Cover box and lid with decorative Con-Tact paper, or cover with white Con-Tact paper and decorate with stickers or permanent markers.

2. Fill box with appropriate shape props.

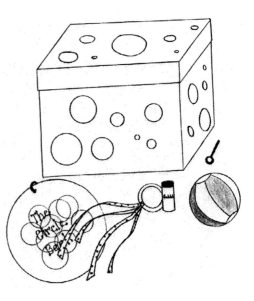

STRETCHER

Waving Shapes

Special Needs

Toddler

Transition Strategy

Toddlers love having something to hold onto and to wave in the air, especially if each child in the group can hold onto her own prop. Vinyl Waving Shapes are soft, pliable, inexpensive shapes cut out of old tablecloths. It's easy to cut any shape, depending on the unit you are working on, out of a variety of colorful tablecloths. You can also cut shapes from colored page protectors. Made of transparent plastic and very durable, this flexible shape will be very appealing to children to wave in the air. Have children hold onto their shapes and sing the following song to the tune of "If You're Happy and You Know It":

> Put your star in the air, in the air.
> Put your star in the air, in the air.
> Put your star in the air and keep it right there.
> Put your star in the air, in the air.

Make up verses using any shape desired and place the shape anywhere desired, such as:

> Put your circle under your foot, under your foot …
> Put your square between your legs, between your legs …
> Put your diamond on your elbow, on your elbow …

It's a great way to reinforce position concepts like over, under, between, and on.

Variation

* **Excuser:** Hand out a variety of shapes and colors. When each child has a shape, say, "If you have the red star (or green square, or yellow circle) you can go wash your hands for lunch." Have children hand you the shapes as they leave.

Materials

Vinyl tablecloth or colored page protectors

Directions

Cut geometric shapes out of tablecloth or page protectors, making them approximately 5–6 inches wide. You can make many of one shape so that every child has the same shape, or a variety of shapes so that each child has a different shape.

Musical 3-D Shapes

Special Needs
Toddler

Transition Strategy:

This stretcher activity is an adaptation of the well-known party game musical chairs. This version allows all children to remain in the game and stretch their muscles when the music stops. Large three-dimensional shapes (made from 2-inch-thick foam) are used instead of chairs. To play the game, the teacher places the foam geometric shapes either in a circle or scattered throughout the group area. Music is then played, and the children walk or tiptoe around the shapes. When the music stops, each child finds a shape and places his or her toe on the shape. If the children are barefooted or in stocking feet, they will enjoy squishing their toes into the foam. The teacher then rolls a Velcro fabric cube that has matching shapes attached. When a shape is rolled, the teacher instructs the children on the corresponding 3-D shape to move in a certain way such as to hop up and down or twirl around. Do this for 5–10 seconds and then put the music on again for the entire group to resume moving around the shapes. The children will want to play this over and over again. The foam shapes are washable, so they can also be taken outside to use on the playground or at the park.

Materials

2-inch-thick foam sheets (available in fabric stores), enough to cut out six 2-by-2-foot shapes
Medium-tip permanent marker
Electric knife
Looped fabric cube (see appendix F)
Art foam, 2 or 3 sheets, or 2–3 vinyl place mats
Adhesive-backed Velcro pieces (hooked side only)
Optional: Wide-tip permanent markers of assorted colors

Directions

3-D Foam Shape

1. Use the medium-tip permanent marker to draw geometric shapes (circle, square, triangle, rectangle, etc.) approximately 2 by 2 feet each, onto one side of the foam.
2. Using an electric knife, cut out each shape. Cut the foam by holding the knife as straight up and down as possible to make a straight edge on the side of the shape.
3. Optional: Decorate the shapes with the wide-tip permanent markers if desired.

Shapes for Looped Fabric Cube

1. On the back of either art foam or vinyl place mats, draw 4-to-6-inch shapes that correspond to the large foam shapes. Cut out the shapes.
2. Attach several pieces of adhesive-backed hooked Velcro onto the back of each shape.
3. Place one shape on each side of the Velcro fabric cube. Your shape cube is ready to use.

EXTENDER

Shape Photo Book

Transition Strategy

Everyone loves photographs, and there is no easier way to fill extra time with kids than by letting them look at photos in this homemade Shape Photo Book. These shape books help teach that there are shapes all around us in our world. Take photos of things in the environment that are a specific shape, such as a rectangular door, a square window, or a circular clock. Draw the shape on a page and then place three or four photos around the drawn shape. The book is made with inexpensive materials, so if young hands inadvertently rip a page—no problem! It can be replaced at very little cost.

Variation

★ **Magic Carpet Activity:** These homemade photo books make a great addition to your Magic Carpet shelf. Make enough books so that every two children can share one book. Make a variety of books for different shapes.

Materials

Clear page protectors (8½ by 11 inches)
Three 1-inch metal rings
File folders
Photos of objects in the environment that illustrate different shapes, or calendar pictures

Directions

1. Cut file folders to fit inside page protectors.
2. Draw a shape onto the center of each page made from a file folder. Glue shape photos or calendar pictures of similar shapes around drawn shapes.
3. Slide each page inside a page protector.
4. Design one page to be the cover. Title the book something like "Our Circle Book!"
5. Connect pages with metal rings.

Who Has the Shape?

Special Needs

Toddler

Transition Strategy

Keep children busy guessing who has the pillow. You can make these simple shape pillows by sewing or gluing pieces of material together and filling with polyester fill. Have the children sit in a circle, hold their hands behind their backs, and close their eyes. Quietly place the pillow in the hands of one of the children and sing (to the tune "Row, Row, Row Your Boat")

> Who has it, who has it, who has the little (heart)?
> Who has it, who has it, who has the little (heart)?

The children then take turns guessing who has the hidden shape.

Variations

★ **Routine Change:** These shapes are great to use for routine changes because toddlers love little objects they can tuck in their hands. Make enough so everyone can have his own. Let toddlers manipulate them while they're being changed or sitting on the potty chair. They will also enjoy carrying the pillows around, wrapping them in a blanket, or tucking them in a fanny pack to take along for a Magical Moment.

★ **Settler:** To help children settle into group time, sing this variation to the song: "Welcome (child's name), you may have the (heart). Welcome (child's name), you may have the heart."

★ **Extender:** Hide several shapes around the room and have the children search until every child finds one shape.

★ **Excuser:** When it's time to excuse the children from group time sing, "Good-bye (child's name), please pass (another child's name) the (heart), good-bye (child's name), you may go outside, go to lunch, get your coat."

★ **Excuser:** To excuse children from a group one at a time, gently toss a shape to one child, saying, "It's Susie's time to get her coat on now." Susie gently tosses the pillow back to the teacher and leaves the group. This continues until all the children are excused.

Materials

Vinyl tablecloth or felt pieces, 5–6 inches square
Polyester stuffing
Craft glue or sewing thread
Optional: ¼-inch ribbon or lace

Directions

1. Draw the desired shape on a piece of tablecloth or felt and cut out. Holding two pieces together, sew or glue most of the way around the shape, leaving a space for filling with polyester stuffing. If using satin ribbon, use a needle with a large eye and sew the pieces together with a decorative running stitch.

2. Fill with a small amount of polyester stuffing. Then finish gluing or sewing the shape together.

3. If using ribbon, tie the ends into a bow. Or you can decorate by gluing or sewing lace around the edge of the shape.

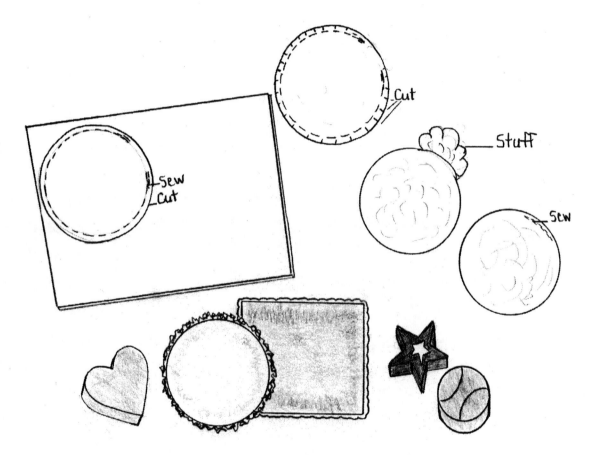

Connect Four

Transition Strategy

Connect Four is an old game that can keep children occupied for long periods of time. This reusable homemade version is so easy to make that you can make several to have on hand for those older preschoolers. To play, children take turns drawing lines to connect two dots. When a square is made, the child connecting the last line puts his initial inside the square. The game continues until all the dots are connected. To start a new game, simply wipe the board clean with a tissue and start again.

Materials

Poster board or file
  folder
Small shape stickers
  (such as hearts
  or sticky dots)
  or nonperma-
  nent markers
Clear Con-Tact
  paper
Overhead trans-
  parency markers
Tissues
Small plastic bags
Brass paper
  fastener

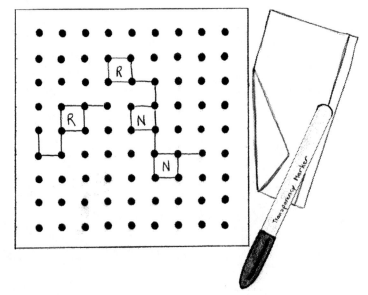

Directions

1. Cut the poster board or file folder into a square (approximately 10 by 10 inches).

2. Place stickers in five rows of five each, so that the stickers are evenly spaced (see illustration), or use nonpermanent markers to draw small dots in the same pattern described above.

3. Cover with clear Con-Tact paper.

4. Place overhead transparency marker and tissues in a small plastic bag. Attach to a corner of the Connect Four board with the paper fastener.

Bucket of Magnetic Circles

Transition Strategy

This little bucket of metal caps will be so popular, you'll want to have several available for your class. So start saving those drink caps today! And the game is so very simple to assemble. The bucket is just an old peanut-butter container decorated with stickers. It is filled with the metal caps (also decorated with stickers) that come on bottles of juice or the metal lids from cans of frozen juice concentrate. The latter are good for toddlers because they clearly pass the "choke-tube test." Place a magnetic wand alongside the bucket and watch the children become captivated dipping the wand into the bucket to see how many caps "stick" to the wand. The noise and feel of the caps will appeal to toddlers (and all ages!). If colored sticky dots are placed on the caps or lids, children can sort into similar groups or match similar stickers. Two children can play together by taking turns pulling lids out of the bucket.

Variation

★ **Excuser:** Place colored sticky dots on the metal caps. Put one of each color in the bucket. Excuse children from group time by pulling one cap out at a time and announcing that every child wearing that color can leave.

Shape-Matching Cards

Transition Strategy

These versatile matching boards can be made in countless number of ways depending on the ages and needs of the children you work with. Shape-Matching Cards are simply cards divided into two sides with shapes on both sides for matching. The left side has one shape (either a hand-drawn shape or a sticker); the right side has two or more shapes. The child must find a shape on the right side that matches the shape on the left side. Older preschoolers can handle more choices, so the right-hand boards can have five or more shapes. Place cards of varying levels of difficulty together in a basket and let children choose their own cards. Using overhead transparency markers, children can either circle the correct choice(s) or draw a line between the matching shapes. Transparency markers wipe off easily with a damp tissue. Just put a marker and several tissues in a small self-sealing plastic bag and store it in the basket with the Shape-Matching Cards.

Variation

Have children connect the shapes with a rubber band. Simply insert a brass paper fastener to the right of each shape or sticker. Slip a rubber band around the paper fastener on the left side of the card. Push the paper fastener down so that the rubber band fits snugly under it. On the back of the card, open the fastener and tape over it to secure it. To play the game, the child matches the shapes and slips the rubber band around the fastener next to the matching shape on the right side of the board.

Materials

Poster board or file folders
Water-base markers (permanent marker bleeds through contact paper over time)
Variety of shapes or decorative stickers
Clear Con-Tact paper
Overhead-transparency markers
Small resealable plastic bags
Tissues

Directions

1. Cut poster board or file folders into any size desired. (Hint: Cutting them 8½ by 11 inches or smaller makes them easier to store.)

2. Draw a line vertically across the board dividing the space into two parts. It can be divided in half or into ⅓ and ⅔ sections depending on the number of shapes being put on the right side.

3. Draw one shape or place one sticker on the left side of the board. Draw two or more shapes, or place two or more stickers, on the right side of the board. One or more of the shapes on the right should match the shape on the left (see illustration for examples).

4. Cover with clear Con-Tact paper.

5. Place overhead-transparency marker and tissues in plastic bags and either attach to individual boards with a piece of Velcro, or store in basket with the boards.

Picking Up Shapes

Special Needs

Toddler

Transition Strategy

When you are working on a certain shape in your classroom and just want to have a fun "magical" time, try this easy little activity. Make a variety of shapes out of whatever material you have available (poster board, felt, heavyweight interfacing, or vinyl). Hide the shapes throughout the room or playground. Give each child in your class a little basket and send her out to pick up shapes. Place the shapes in easy view for toddlers; with preschoolers, on the other hand, you can get quite tricky. Even children with attention difficulties will spend a good amount of time on this search. This doesn't have to be part of group time. It's just one of those little magical extras that add a little zip to your day.

Variation:

★ **Magical Moment:** Have children form a circle. Choose a child to pick up some shapes (one at a time) from a basket while you sing this song to the tune "Picking Up Paw Paws": "Picking up (hearts) and putting them in a basket, picking up (hearts) and putting them in the basket. Picking up (hearts) and putting them in the basket." Choose another child and sing again. Continue until all the shapes are picked up.

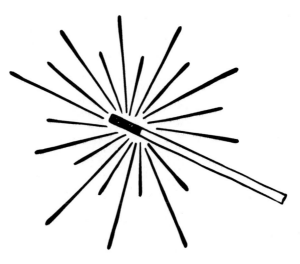

MAGICAL
MOMENT

Bag-o-Buttons

Transition Strategy

If you suddenly find yourself with a few minutes to fill, just pull out this bag full of large plastic craft buttons, which come in assorted colors and geometric shapes. Children will immediately be attracted by the bright, colorful shapes. Have a child pull one button out of the bag, then ask all the children to look around to find something nearby which is the same shape as the button. In no time at all they will be discovering that shapes aren't just something to draw on a paper—that everything has a shape. The bag is small and lightweight, perfect to carry along on field trips, on visits to the library, or to the park.

Materials

Large plastic shape buttons (available in craft stores or craft sections
of discount stores)
1 felt rectangle (standard size, 9 by 12 inches)
Brightly colored ribbon or shoelace (18–24 inches long)
Small safety pin
Optional: Fabric paints in assorted colors
Sewing machine

Directions

Button Bag

1. Fold piece of felt crosswise in half so that it becomes a 6-by-9-inch rectangle. Sew along the bottom and open side of the rectangle to make a small bag.
    Do NOT sew across the top.

2. Fold the top edge down 1 inch. Sew along the bottom edge of the folded-down top, making a tube to insert the ribbon or shoelace.
    Leave a small opening to insert the ribbon or shoelace.

3. Pin the safety pin onto one end of the ribbon or shoelace. Insert the pin end of the ribbon or shoelace into the opening of the tube and, using the pin to push with, push the ribbon all the way through the tube and pull it through the opening. Pull the ribbon or shoelace so that there is an equal amount on both sides extending from the bag. Remove the safety pin. Tie a knot at each end or knot the ends together so that the ribbon doesn't slide back into the bag.

4. Turn the bag right side out.

5. Optional: Decorate the outside of the bag by painting geometric shapes in assorted colors in a random fashion on the bag.

6. When the paint is dry, fill the bag with purchased shape buttons.

EXCUSER

Names on Notepads

Transition Strategy

When children are eager to move on to the next activity on the schedule, such as going to lunch or outside to the playground, it can be very difficult for them to sit and wait to hear their names called. Having something to look at or watch for will help them through this. Teacher-supply stores and discount stores are full of memo pads in many shapes and sizes. Write each child's name on one piece of memo paper, and cover each piece with Con-Tact paper. You can make a different set of names to match any theme you may do.

Variations

* **Stretcher:** Use the Con-Tact paper covered shapes as props for a stretching activity. Have the children swing or sway while holding a shape. Or have them move around shapes that you have attached to the floor with Con-Tact paper.

* **Extender:** Attach shapes around the room (on the walls, backs of shelves, doors, chairs, or ceilings) with clear Con-Tact paper. When you need to extend a group time, ask children to look around and find a shape. Have them raise their hands or point to the shape when they find one.

* **Magical Moment:** Toddlers love to look at and name the shapes during wait times. Several could be attached on the wall and floor around the potty chair or changing table. They make good conversation starters.

Materials

Shape note pad (of any desired shape or size)
Water-base marker
Clear Con-Tact paper

Directions

1. Print each child's name on one sheet of notepad paper with the non-permanent marker (permanent will bleed through the Con-Tact paper over time).

2. Cover the notepad paper with clear Con-Tact paper.

EXCUSER

Pass the Shape

Transition Strategy

Children love to touch things with interesting textures, so this sponge shape on a pencil will be a big hit in your classroom. When it's time to excuse the children from a group, help them take turns leaving by passing around this prop. Just hand the shape on the stick to the first child, announcing that it's her turn to move on to the next activity. This child then passes the shape on to another child and announces that it's his turn to leave. Encourage children to get up and walk to the child they are choosing. This activity continues until all the children have left the group. The shape on the stick will be so appealing to children that they will want to hang onto it for a few minutes before passing it on. By simply sticking foam shapes onto the ends of pencils, you can make a variety of shapes to have on hand.

Variation

★ **Routine Change:** Announce routine changes by speaking into the shape on the stick as if it were a microphone. Give children a chance to be the announcers too.

Materials

Sponge (or foam) shape (available in craft stores for stenciling)
Cute pencil
Optional: craft glue

Directions

1. With the scissors tips, cut a small hole into the bottom of the foam shape.

2. Insert the lead end of the pencil snugly into the hole. If the foam comes off easily, you might want to put a small amount of craft glue into the hole before inserting the pencil.

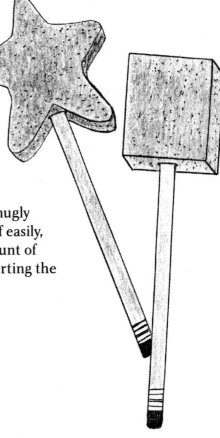

Appendix A: Glossary

Attention-deficit/hyperactivity disorder (AD/HD)—A neurological disorder that involves inappropriate behavior including poor attention skills, impulsivity, and hyperactivity.

Attention grabbers—Interesting objects or brief activities designed to get and focus children's attention. Present them with a little suspense, surprise, or mystery for greatest attention-getting results.

Autism—A neurological or brain disorder that can affect social interacion and communication skills as well as the ability to engage in imaginative play. This developmental disorder usually becomes evident before age three.

Bag of tricks—Collection of quick and amusing learning activities to facilitate transitions with children.

Best practices—The most appropriate ways to teach and guide children.

Classroom setting—The general term used in this book for the environment of early-childhood programs.

Concept—A basic fact or idea grasped by the mind such as numbers, colors, or shapes.

Con-Tact paper—Self-adhesive covering of clear, colored, or patterned plastic.

Daily schedule—The order and time spans of activities and routines throughout the day.

Developmental area—A way of organizing the clusters of skills children learn as they develop. Common developmental areas include cognitive, social/emotional, physical/motor, communication/language, and self-help.

Developmentally Appropriate Practice (DAP)—Guideline for providing a developmentally appropriate program for children from birth through eight years, set forth in a series of position papers published by The National Association for the Education of Young Children (NAEYC), 1986.

Dramatic play—Symbolic play in which children take on the roles of people and animals and interact in various play situations such as family life, doctor's office, or grocery shopping.

"Drop and flop" time—A time in which teachers of toddlers offer to read, sing, or do activities with individuals or small groups. Toddlers choose whether to participate in "drop and flop" times.

Early childhood education (ECE)—Programs for children ages birth to five years, including but not limited to family child care, child care centers, Head Start, kindergartens, and half-day preschool classrooms.

Emergent curriculum—An approach to curriculum in which a topic *emerges* from children's interests and is sustained for as long as the interest continues.

Emergent transitions—Transitions planned and carried out according to the topic being taught and the children's abilities, interests, and needs. Transitions are used as long as they are effective and then changed to revitalize the routines.

Excusers—Methods and activities used to dismiss children from a group activity and transition them to another activity.

Extenders—Activities that extend the time when you have a few minutes to fill or expand children's knowledge about a current theme or a previously learned topic.

Finger plays—Simple rhymes that are spoken or chanted, dramatized by finger and hand motions.

Free choice time—A period of the day in which children choose among different activities and make decisions about their level of participation.

Group time—An all-class gathering for guided, teacher-directed activities.

Guidance—Direction and training of behavior, emphasizing encouragement, with the goal that children will develop self-control; for many teachers, this term replaces the more negative concept of "discipline."

Inclusive classroom—Program that includes all children even if they have disabilities.

Interest centers—Activity areas that respond to the children's interests and developmental needs. Children can choose what they want to do and how long they wish to spend in the center.

Laminate—To encase a piece of paper in thin sheets of clear plastic which are applied by a machine using heat.

Looped fabric—Various fabrics, including Headliner, Tempo, indoor-outdoor carpeting, and Velcro.

Magical Moments—Times when a group of children are between activities, on the move, or out of the room. The teacher makes creative use of the environment and of small portable materials to occupy children in a productive manner.

Magic Carpet activities—Learning activities done in a designated "magic carpet" place while waiting for others to finish a task. Many are self-contained activities used individually. Other activities are cooperative in nature and are used by pairs of children.

Magician's Map—A "web" of transition activities and how they relate to each other; can be based on an emergent topic or a planned theme. See the beginning of each chapter for a map showing how activities in that chapter relate to each other. The map helps a teacher arrive at concepts, activities, and transitions.

Magnetic board—A metal surface that attracts and holds magnetic pieces.

National Association for the Education of Young Children (NAEYC)—A professional organization for people working with young children.

No-choke testing tube—A tube used to measure small items to determine whether or not they are small enough to cause a child to choke. Available in most early childhood catalogs.

Poster board—A lightweight cardboard available in a variety of colors. Also called *tag board.*

Props—Tangibles and visual aids used to accompany teaching activities.

Preschoolers—Children ages three to five years.

Push-button music box—Small, inexpensive music disc activated by pushing the surface of the button.

Routine—A procedure within a daily schedule that is consistently followed. In a child care setting, typical routine activities are arrival, breakfast, snack, lunch, handwashing, toileting, diaper changing, naptime or rest time, and departure.

Routine changes—Techniques used to signal a change in the routine from one activity to the next. Along with verbal direction, a variety of sensory cues are used to signal the change to the children.

Sensory integration—The way in which the brain sorts out multiple sensory perceptions. Children with a disability in this area can have particular difficulty with transitions between activities.

Settlers—Techniques used to gather children together, quiet them, and prepare them for group time.

Sit-upon—Teacher-made cushion, pad, or mat on which a child can sit.

Spray adhesive—Glue sprayed from an aerosol can, found in craft stores.

Stencil-cutting machine—A machine that cuts various shapes, letters, and numbers. Also called a *die-cut machine*. One brand name is The Ellison Letter Machine.

Stiffened felt—A fabric found in craft or fabric stores. Similar fabrics include pennant material and heavyweight interfacing. Milk filters for milking machines can also be used; they are sold in farm-implement stores.

Stretchers—Exercises that get children and staff moving and stretching, often needed for a change of pace or to expend pent-up energy.

Tactile—Involving the sense of touch.

Toddlers—Children ages one to three years.

Topic—The curriculum focus for learning; may be determined by the children's interests, the teacher's plans, or both.

Transition—Children's movement from one activity or routine to another. The transition becomes an activity itself if planned and facilitated.

Triple-A (Anticipate, Act, and Avert)—A strategy to help teachers guide children's behavior. First, *anticipate* times and situations that children will need teacher guidance. Then, *act* by making changes in the environment or using transitional activities. Anticipating and acting will *avert* behavior problems and ease the transition.

Velcro—A brand name for loop-and-hook fastener fabric, available in strips and other forms, with or without adhesive backing.

Vis A Vis Marker—A brand name for a marker used to write on overhead transparencies, write-and-wipe boards, or Con-Tact paper.

Wait time—The time children have to wait while their classmates finish an activity or routine, before another activity or routine begins.

Appendix B: References and Resources

References

Benson McMullen, M. "Achieving Best Practices in Infant and Toddler Care and Education." *Young Children,* July 1999.

Bredekamp, S., and Copple, C., ed. *Developmentally Appropriate Practice in Early Childhood Programs.* Revised Edition. Washington, DC: National Association for the Education of Young Children, 1997.

Jones, E., and Nimmo, J. *Emergent Curriculum.* Washington, DC: National Association for the Education of Young Children, 1994.

Kaiser, B., and Sklar Rasminsky, J. *Meeting the Challenge.* Ottawa, Ontario: Canadian Child Care Federation, 1999.

Larson, N., Henthone, M., and Plum, B. *Transition Magician: Guiding Young Children in Early Childhood Classrooms.* St. Paul: Redleaf Press, 1994.

Teacher Resources

Children's Books

Allen, Constance. *Sesame Street ABC.* Audiotape. Sony Wonder, 1996.

Baker, Keith. *Hide and Snake.* New York: The Trumpet Club, 1991.

Carle, Eric. *The Very Hungry Caterpillar.* New York: Philomel Books, 1987.

Carle, Eric. *The Very Quiet Cricket.* New York: Philomel Books, 1997.

Carle, Eric. *The Grouchy Ladybug.* New York: HarperCollins, 1996.

Carle, Eric. *The Very Busy Spider.* New York: Philomel Books, 1984.

Carle, Eric. *The Mixed Up Chameleon.* New York: HarperCollins, 1998.

Martin, Bill. *Brown Bear, Brown Bear, What Do You See?* New York: H. Holt, 1996.

Slobodkina, Esphyr. *Caps for Sale.* Menlo Park, CA: Addison Wesley, 1940.

Walsh, Ellen S. *Mouse Count.* San Diego: Trumpet, 1991.

Resource Books

Catlin, Cynthia. *More Toddlers Together.* Beltsville, MD: Gryphon House, 1996.

Christoph, J., and Wagonseller, B. *A Teacher's Fix-It Yourself ADHD Manual.* Chicago: United Learning, 1998.

Curtis, Deb, and Carter, Margie. *Reflecting Children's Lives.* Saint Paul: Redleaf Press, 1996.

Deiner, Penny. *Resources for Educating Children with Diverse Abilities Birth through Eight.* Harcourt Brace College Publishers, 1999.

Frick, Sheila. *Out of the Mouths of Babes.* (Sensory integration) Hugo, MN: POP Press, 1996.

Gould, Patti, and Sullivan, Joyce. *The Inclusive Early Childhood Classroom.* Beltsville, MD: Gryphon House, 1999.

James, Beverly. *Treating Traumatized Children New Insights and Creative Interventions.* New York: The Free Press, 1989.

Jones, Clare. *Sourcebook for Children with Attention Deficit Disorder.* San Antonio: Communication Skill Builders, 1991.

Larson, N., Henthorne, M., and Plum, B. *Transition Magician: Strategies to Guide Young Children in Early Childhood Programs.* St. Paul: Redleaf Press, 1994.

McGinnis, E., and Goldstein. *Skillstreaming in Early Childhood Education: Teaching ProSocial Skills to the Preschool and Kindergarten Child.* Champaign, IL: Research Press Co., 1990.

Monahan, C. *Children and Trauma: A Guide for Parents and Professionals.* San Francisco: Jossey-Bass, 1993.

Redleaf, Rhoda, and Robertson, Audrey. *Learn and Play the Recycle Way.* St. Paul: Redleaf Press, 1999.

Riekehof, Lottie L. *The Joy of Signing.* Springfield, MO: Gospel Publishing House, 1985.

Sher, Barbara. *Extraordinary Play with Ordinary Things.* Holbrook, MA: Bob Adams, Inc., 1994.

Siegel, B. *The World of the Autistic Child.* New York: Oxford University Press, 1996.

Silberg, Jackie. *Games to Play with Toddlers.* Mt. Rainier, MD: Gryphon House, 1993.

Silberg, Jackie. *Games to Play with Two Year Olds.* Beltsville, MD: Gryphon House, 1994.

Silberg, Jackie. *500 Five-Minute Games.* Beltsville, MD: Gryphon House, 1995.

Swee Hong, Chia. *Sensory Motor Activities for Early Development.* Oxon, UK: Winslow, 1996.

Wilmes, Liz and Dick. *2's Experience Sensory Play.* Elgin, IL: Building Blocks Publications, 1996.

Music

Ambrose Brazelton. *Clap Snap and Tap.* Educational Activities, Inc., 1973.

Virginia Dixon. *Classical Music.* Twin Sisters Productions, 1998.

Colleen Hannafin and Brian Schellinger. *Colleen and Uncle Squaty.* Eau Claire, WI: Green Meadow Production on Nice Skies Tapes, 1993. (800-828-9046)

Gentle Persuasion: The Sounds of Nature, Sounds and Songs of the Humpback Whales. Audiotape or CD. Englewood, CA: The Special Music Co., 1989

Otis, Johnny. *The Heart 'n' Soul of Rock 'n' Roll.* Reader's Digest Association, 1987.

Bev Bos, Michael Leeman, and Tom Hunter. *I Have a Box.* Roseville, CA: Turn-the-Page Press, 1995.

Me and My Bean Bag—The Learning Station. Long Branch, NJ: Kimbo Educational, 1988.

Hap Palmer. *Movin'.* Freeport, NY: Educational Activities, Inc., 1973.

Frank Mills. *Music Box Dancer.* New York: Polydor, Inc., 1979.

Stewart, Georgiana. *Bean Bag Activities & Coordination Skills for Early Childhood.* Long Branch, NJ: Kimbo Educational.

Gary Lamb. Sixty Beats Per Minute Tapes and CDs. Includes *The Language of Love, Twelve Promises, A Walk in the Garden, Watching the Night Fall.* Santa Cruz, CA: Gary Lamb Music. P.O. Box 4100, Santa Cruz, CA 95063. http://www.garylamb.com

Greg Scelsa and Steve Millang. *We All Live Together,* Volume 4. Youngheart Records, 1980.

Suppliers

Creative Educational Surplus: Now affiliated with Discount School Supplies.

Discount School Supplies, P.O. Box 7636, Spreckels, CA 93962-7636, (800-627-2829), www.earlychildhood.com

Ellison Educational Equipment, Inc., P.O. Box 8209, Newport Beach, CA 92658-8209 (800-253-2238). Source for The Ellison Letter Machine.

InnerPlay, 17290 Circle Drive, Lakewood, WI 54138 (715-276-3338)

Oriental Trading Company, Inc., P.O. Box 2318, Omaha, NE 68103-2318.

U.S. Toy Company, 13201 Arrington Road, Grandview, MO 64030 (800-255-6124), ustoy@ustoyco.com

Appendix C: Forms for Evaluation and Reflection

Classroom Evaluation Scale

DIRECTIONS: Using a scale of 1 to 5, rate your classroom by circling the appropriate number. Circle 2 or 4 if you think your classroom falls in between the stated criteria.

Selecting Materials

1	2	3	4	5
An insufficient number of toys and pieces of equipment per child. Or all toys and equipment owned by the center are out, with none in reserve. Materials are not rotated. There are many broken or incomplete toy sets. Room is overfilled with colorful materials, which can be distracting. Toys with small pieces are within reach of infants and toddlers.		A sufficient number of toys, but a limited variety. Occasionally a new toy or piece of equipment is added.		An option-filled environment. Activities and materials are selected based on the children's needs and interests. A range of developmental play choices are provided each day. Learning centers provide opportunities to play alone, with another child, or with several children under the teacher's guidance. Accommodations have been made for varying ages and abilities. Consideration has been given to the needs of children who are easily distracted. Materials that are potential choking hazards are out of reach of toddlers and infants. Enough materials are provided that toddlers don't have to share.

Developmental Appropriateness

1	2	3	4	5
Children are either bored or frustrated by the toys and activities because they are too simple or too complex. No guidance for selection is provided. Activities are planned at one skill level.		Activities are planned for a range of skills and abilities but not on a consistent basis. Little individualizing of activities is done. There are too many toys on shelves for toddlers, and toys are not rotated often.		Toys and activities are appropriate for a range of developmental levels. Activities for children with varying abilities are planned. Teachers guide children to appropriate toys and activities. The number of toys on shelves for toddlers is limited, and toys are rotated often as children tire of them. Toys and activities focus on strengths of children with varying abilities.

Accessibility / Storage

1	2	3	4	5
Supplies are kept in closed cupboards or up high. Teacher assistance is necessary. Toys and materials are placed in one container or box. Toys do not have a specified place on the shelf. Dress-up clothes are stored in a box.		Toy bins are unlabeled. Storage shelves for some toys are accessible to children. Teacher assistance is required for some items such as books, paints, and scissors, which are stored out of reach. Teacher materials are generally out of sight and reach.		The majority of materials and equipment are accessible to the children. Materials are stored on low, open shelves; toys and materials have a place; containers and shelves are coded so children can get and return items. Accessible personal space is provided for children's belongings, identified with children's names. Teacher storage is clearly defined for children.

Room Arrangement

1	2	3	4	5
Arrangement of the room creates congested pathways; traffic patterns cut through play areas or create open space that invites running.		The room has identified learning centers, but little attention has been paid to balancing active and quiet play areas. Pathways are narrowly defined, and children can't see from one play area to another.		Equipment and interest centers are arranged so children can move easily from one area to another. Individual and quiet activities are placed together and away from traffic flow. Noisy, active centers are placed close to each other. There is a balance of active and quiet activities. There is plenty of space for children in wheelchairs to move freely throughout the room and in centers.

Large-Group Area

1	2	3	4	5
Toys and bookshelves surround the large-group space. Children look out at the full classroom or toward the doorway. Little or no thought is given to sitting surfaces for children.		Group time focuses toward the teacher or is situated in a corner of the room. Some care is taken to drape open shelves on either side of the group area.		Group-time space is placed out of the flow of traffic and away from toys and bookshelves. A carpet (or individual sitting places) defines the group area. The teacher brings to the group area only the things she expects children to focus on, plus materials for wait time. Accommodation has been made for children with attention difficulties (e.g., bean bags or rocking chairs added).

Play Spaces

1	2	3	4	5
Learning centers are not clearly defined. Children don't have a sense of being in a certain center. Centers are often crowded. Children seem disoriented or confused and sometimes aggressive as a result of the crowding.		Limited number of learning centers is provided. Any number of children can play in a given space, or teacher closely regulates number of children in centers. Boundaries are not always clear. There is no space to be alone.		Spaces are provided where the entire class can gather or where children can play in groups of two to four children. There is space where a child can be alone. Ample space is provided in learning centers such as the block and dramatic-play areas. The room is organized in clearly defined areas. Each area is pictorially labeled. Low dividers, shelves, or pieces of carpet define areas. Children can self-regulate movement between play areas. Interest centers are set up for total inclusion.

Supervision

1	2	3	4	5
Some play areas are not visible to teachers. Teachers congregate in one area, leaving other parts of the room unsupervised.		Teachers are present to oversee activities but seldom get directly involved. Staff occasionally scans the room.		Equipment and furniture are arranged so that children are easily observed. Low shelves or dividers are used. Teachers move about the room as children play and are available to observe and guide. Teachers are aware of where children are in the room.

After completing the rating scale, ask yourself these questions:

⭐ **1**

Do I provide an option-filled environment?	YES	NO	
Do I know children's interests?	YES	NO	SOMETIMES
Do I provide thoughtful play choices based on children's current interests?	YES	NO	SOMETIMES

For example, if children are interested in writing, do I provide a writing table with pencils, paper, envelopes, stencils, etc.?

What changes could I make?

_____

_____

_____

⭐ **2**

Each day, do children have opportunities to play alone?	YES	NO
With one or two others?	YES	NO
In a large group?	YES	NO

_____

_____

_____

⭐ **3**

Do I consider children's developmental needs (social, emotional, cognitive, and physical) when I prepare the environment?　　YES　NO　SOMETIMES

Write examples here.

_____

_____

_____

⭐ **4**

Do I provide manipulatives such as puzzles for all skill levels, from knobbed four-piece puzzles to fifteen-piece puzzles for more skilled children?　　YES　NO

Write other examples here.

_____

_____

_____

⭐ **5**

Do I plan activities that I can adapt for the lowest-functioning child to the highest-functioning child?　　YES　NO

Write some examples here.

_____

_____

_____

★ **6** In my classroom, do I promote a child's self-esteem by providing activities in which the child will experience success several times each day?   YES   NO   SOMETIMES

Do my activities respect children's growing independence?   YES   NO   SOMETIMES

Write some examples here.

_____

_____

_____

★ **7** Do I encourage independence during choice time and routine times?   YES   NO

Can children get materials out and return them properly to shelves without my assistance?   YES   NO

Write your own examples of encouraging independence here.

How could I improve on this?

_____

_____

_____

★ **8** Is my classroom arranged so children can move easily from one learning center to another?   YES   NO

Are learning centers clearly defined?   YES   NO

How can I improve this?

_____

_____

_____

★ **9** Do I move about the room observing children as they play?   YES   NO   SOMETIMES

Do I cover unattended parts of the room when my teaching partner is involved with the other children?   YES   NO

If necessary, do I guide children's play or become actively involved?   YES   NO   SOMETIMES

_____

_____

_____

★ **10** Does my group-time area have clearly defined and comfortable seating for children?   YES   NO

Is my group area free of unnecessary distractions?   YES   NO

How might I change it to help children focus better?

_____

_____

_____

Reflection: Setting the Stage

The following activity will help you pinpoint areas of the classroom where the most frequent disputes or disruptions occur.

Room Arrangement Observation

In the space below, draw a simple floor plan of your classroom. Include all interest areas, equipment, and furniture. Show everything, including bathrooms, cubby areas, windows, and doors.

Post your floor plan in a convenient location in your room for one week. On the floor plan, indicate with an X the areas where any disruptions occur. A disruption is an incident that children cannot resolve on their own but need a teacher to assist them. Color code the Xs to indicate disruptions that happened in the morning and ones that happened in the afternoon.

Make a photocopy of the page for observation purposes.

Reflection

After a week, look at your floor plan and identify problem areas. Then review the classroom evaluation scale at the beginning of this appendix. Look at each category (selecting materials, developmental appropriateness, accessibility/storage, and so on). List any problems from the first two columns that are contributing to problem areas identified in your classroom.

Changes I need to make:

_____

_____

_____

_____

_____

_____

_____

_____

_____

_____

_____

_____

_____

_____

_____

_____

_____

_____

_____

_____

_____

_____

Juggling Your Day

The following activity will help you examine your present schedule. When completed, this observation will indicate which times of the day are most difficult for your group.

My Daily Schedule Observation

Write your daily schedule in the space below. Post your schedule in a convenient location in your room for one week. Indicate with an X any time during the day when children's behavior is particularly chaotic or disruptive and/or requires teacher assistance. You may want to use a different color for each day.

My Daily Schedule

Copy completed page and post it in your room.

Reflection

After a week's observation, identify the problem times in your schedule. Ask yourself these questions and circle your answers. (If you do not wish to write in this book, photocopy this page to use for your evaluation.)

1. Did I find trouble spots in my schedule?   YES   NO

2. Where are my trouble spots? Which routine is most difficult?

    _____

    _____

    _____

    _____

3. What is causing the trouble? (Is it length of the activity, lack of active involvement of children, etc.?)

    _____

    _____

    _____

    _____

4. Are my expectations clear?   YES   NO

5. Do I explain the transition, give children a warning, etc.?   YES   NO

6. Are there too many transitions?   YES   NO

7. Are waiting times during transitions too long?   YES   NO

8. Is there enough adult supervision?   YES   NO

9. Are problems due to poor planning?   YES   NO

10. Was I able to pinpoint my trouble spots?   YES   NO

©2000 *Transition Magician 2*; Redleaf Press, 10 Yorkton Court, St. Paul, MN 55117, 800-423-8309

My Plan of Action

Make a plan to change your room arrangement or schedule. Review your plan after two weeks. (If you do not wish to write in this book, you may photocopy this page.)

Goal 1

_____

Action Steps:

_____
_____
_____

Goal 2

_____

Action Steps:

_____
_____
_____

Goal 3

_____

Action Steps:

_____
_____
_____

Evaluation

Determine if your schedule is developmentally appropriate. Use the appropriate expectations evaluation that follows.

Appropriate Expectations Evaluation

Total the minutes the children spend in each of the following activities during your morning from opening to noon. (Later, evaluate your afternoon schedule as well.) Photocopy this page to use for evaluation purposes.

1. Small-Group Activities   _____

2. Free Choice/Individual Play   _____

3. Outdoor/Large-Motor Activities   _____

4. Large-Group Activities (not including routines)   _____

5. Routines (hand washing, eating, etc.)   _____

Total 1, 2, and 3   _____

Total 4 and 5   _____

Total minutes   _____

Add up the amount of time children spend in:

Teacher-directed activities (including routines if they are

    teacher assisted)   _____

Child-choice activities (including routines done independently)   _____

Total minutes   _____

Evaluation

Examine your daily schedule to determine which transition times are the most difficult for you. Identify those chaotic or difficult transitions by simple observation. Use the following ideas to help you evaluate your transition times.

Transition Observation

Step One: Look at your present schedule and count the number of transitions in your day.

My total is _____.

Step Two: List difficult transition times for you and the children.

_____

_____

_____

_____

_____

Step Three: Count the minutes children have to wait.

In the morning _____

In the afternoon _____

Look at your schedule and estimate the time children must wait during each transition. Start timing at the end of one activity and continue until a new activity begins. (This counting does not have to be exact, only an estimate.)

For example, in one program there are no toileting facilities in the room and the children must walk down the hall to toilet. Children have ten minutes to complete the routine. Most children will have to wait for other children at least six minutes of the ten minutes.

Appendix D:
Master Magician's Map

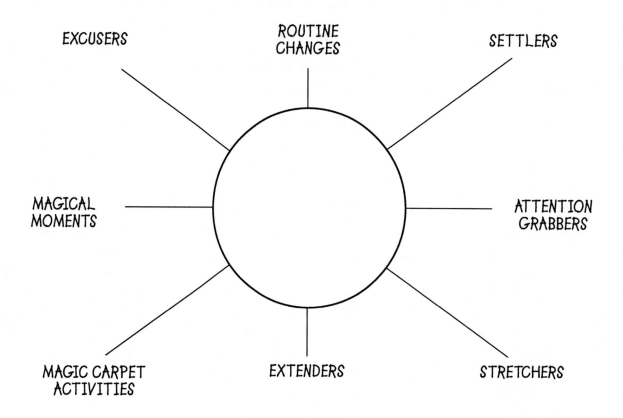

Appendix E: Patterns

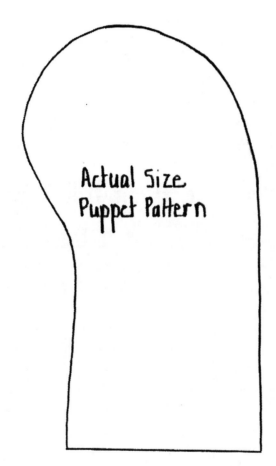

Actual Size
Puppet Pattern

Actual Size Magic Mitt Pattern

Whale Mat Pattern

Appendix F: Directions from *Transition Magician*

Pom-Poms

Although there are pom-pom makers, making your own allows you to choose colors, sizes, and thickness. They take about ten to fifteen minutes to make and provide children with hours of delight.

Variation 1

You will need:

* four-ply or rug yarn
* scissors
* optional: 3″ to 4″ square of thick cardboard

1. Wrap the yarn around the palm of your hand or cut a square piece of cardboard the desired size of your pom-poms (about 3″ to 4″) and wrap the yarn around that. Continue wrapping until you have the desired thickness (about one-third of a typical skein per pom-pom).

2. Pull the yarn off your hand or cardboard, squeezing the center of the loops together.

3. Tightly tie another piece of yarn around the center of the loops. Tie a knot on one side, turn your pom-pom over and tie another knot on the other side, for security.

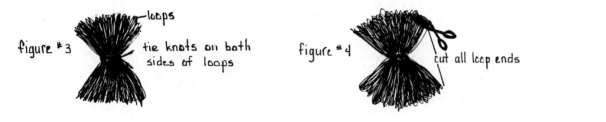

4. Cut all of the loops and shake the pom-pom out.

5. Trim any ragged edges and the yarn that you tied around the center of the loops, forming an evenly rounded ball shape.

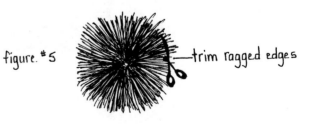

Make several pom-poms. Create multi-colored ones by mixing colors of yarn together. Pull one strand of two or three colors of yarn and wrap them around your hand or cardboard at the same time. This also speeds up the wrapping process.

Variation 2

If you don't want to be bothered with all of the wrapping, try this variation of the pom-pom. Use rug yarn, which is folded perfectly for this variation.

You will need:

* ★ rug yarn
* ★ scissors

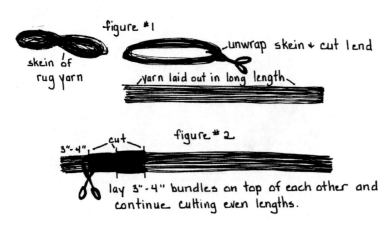

figure #1

skein of rug yarn

unwrap skein + cut 1 end

yarn laid out in long length.

figure #2

3"-4"   cut

lay 3"-4" bundles on top of each other and continue cutting even lengths.

1. Unfold your skein of rug yarn as far as you can so it is laid out in long loops. Then cut one end of the loops. Lay out yarn in long lengths.

2. Choose a length for your pom pom and cut that much yarn (usually 3″ to 4″ long). Place that bundle of yarn on top of the end of the yarn lengths and continue cutting until you have as much yarn in your bundle as you want it thick (usually one-third of the skein).

3. Now gather your large bundle of yarn in your hand, squeezing it together in the middle. Take a separate piece of yarn and tie it tightly around the center of the bundle. Double tying will make it more secure.

figure #3

squeeze together. then tie double knot

4. Shake your bundle out and trim the ragged edges so it is in the form of a nicely rounded ball.

5. Make multi-colored pom-poms with this variation, also. Lay out two or three skeins of different colored yarn and cut your bundles, laying them on top of each other.

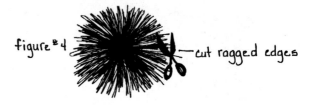

figure #4   — cut ragged edges

figure #5

— red
— white
— blue

Looped Fabric Cube

A looped fabric cube is similar to a large die. The advantage of this item is that pieces are removable. Put different symbols on to fit the concept at hand. Teach children their colors by making stiff Pellon circles of different colors with a strip of hooked fastener on the back. Place the primary colors (red, yellow, and blue) and secondary colors (green, orange, and purple) on the cube. If you are working with older children, put letters of the alphabet onto your cube. There are unlimited possibilities.

You will need

- ★ looped fabric
- ★ polyester stuffing
- ★ stencils for cutting pieces such as numerals, shapes, letters, animals
- ★ material for the pieces such as poster board, rubber place mats, stiff Pellon
- ★ hooked fastener stripping
- ★ sewing machine, needle and thread
- ★ pen or pencil
- ★ scissors
- ★ ruler
- ★ optional: quick bonding glue

The materials listed are for both the looped fabric cube and the hooked fastener pieces.

For the Looped Fabric Cube

1. Cut looped fabric into six equal squares. About 8″ or 9″ squares are a good size.

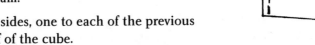

2. Place two squares on top of each other, wrong sides together (loop side out). Machine sew a 1/3″ seam along one side. You want the raw edges on the outside so when you stuff the cube it will maintain its shape. This fabric does not fray. Always double stitch the beginning and the end of the seam.

3. Taking another square, join two sides, one to each of the previous sewn squares. You now have half of the cube.

4. Continue adding squares, sewing them to form a cube. Leave one seam open.

5. Stuff a small amount of polyester stuffing into the open seam. You do not need much because you do not want your cube to bulge out on the sides. If it does bulge, the cube will not land flat on one side when you roll it.

6. With needle and thread, stitch the final seam shut.

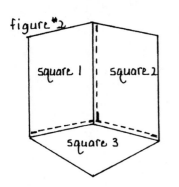

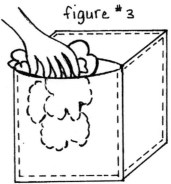

For the Hooked Fastener Pieces

7. Use the stencils to outline pieces of your choice. Use any of the materials listed above, providing they are stiff. Cut out each piece.

8. Adhere small strips of hooked fastener to the back of each piece. The heavier your pieces are, the more hooked fastener you will want to use. For example, on rubber place mats put a small strip on each edge of the piece. You need little on stiff Pellon—just a small strip in the middle of your piece will do the trick.

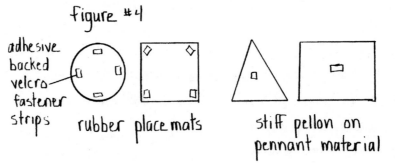

figure #4

adhesive backed velcro fastener strips

rubber place mats

stiff pellon on pennant material

9. If the hooked fastener strips are not sticking, squeeze a small drop of quick bonding glue on the back and position on the piece.

Place your pieces on your cube and you are ready to have loads of fun with this versatile item!

Appendix G: Numbers: Counting in Other Languages

#	Hmong	Spanish	German	French	Italian	Norwegian
1	(ee)-ib	(uno)-uno	(ines)-eins	(ah)-un	(uno)-uno	(ey-in)-en
2	(aw)-ob	(dos)-dos	(zvie)-zwei	(duh)-deux	(do-ay)-due	(toe)-to
3	(bay)-peb	(trays)-tres	(dry)-drei	(twa)-trois)	(tray)-tre	(tray)-tre
4	(blau)-plaub	(quatro)-cuatro	(feer)-fier	(cattra)-quatre	(quat-tro)-quattro	(fee-re)-fire
5	(gee)-tsib	(cinco)-cinco	(funf)-funf	(sank)-cinq	(cheen-quay)-cinque	(fem)-fem
6	(jow)-rau	(says)-seis	(zex)-sechs	(sees)-six	(say)-sei	(sex)-seks
7	(shah)-xya	(siaytay)-siete	(zeebin)-sieben	(set)-sept	(set-tay)-sette	(seev)-syv
8	(yee)-yim	(o-cho)-ocho	(acht)-acht	(wheat)-huit	(otto)-otto	(otta)-åtte
9	(shu-ah)-cuaj	(new-ay-vay)-nueve	(noin)-neun	(nuf)-neuf	(no-vay)-nove	(nee)-ni
10	(gow)-kaum	(dee-ace)-diez	(tzayn)-zehn	(dees)-dix	(dee-ay-chee)-dieci	(tee)-ti

Appendix H

★—Indicates Primary Activity
☆—Indicates Secondary Activity

Activity Name	Toddlers	Kids with Special Needs	Routine Changes	Settlers	Attention Grabbers	Stretchers	Extenders	Magic Carpet Activities	Magical Moments	Excusers
3-D Snow-Person, page 142	✓	✓						★		
ABCs in a Bag, page 71									★	
Accordion Photo Boards, page 109	✓				☆				★	
All-Dressed-Up Puppet, page 42	✓	✓	☆		☆				☆	★
Bag-o-Buttons, page 175		✓							★	
Balloon on a Ring , page 133	✓					★			☆	
Bare-Hand Puppet, page 26	✓				★	☆	☆		☆	☆
Beanbag Bonanza, page 94						★				
Beat the Clock, page 117		✓	★	☆						
Bottle of Names, page 73				☆						★
Box Balancing, page 56	✓				☆	★	☆		☆	
Box-o-Books, page 148								★		
Bubbles on the Go, page 153	✓	✓							★	
Bucket of Magnetic Circles, page 171	✓	✓						★		☆
Clap, Click, and Tap, page 20	✓	✓		★			☆		☆	
Clean-Up Rap, page 116		✓	★							
Clean-Up Signs, page 17		✓	★				☆			
Color Cards, page 138	✓	✓					★		☆	☆
Colorful Water Ring, page 108	✓								★	
Connect Four, page 170								★		
Count the Steps, page 155		✓	☆							★
Counting Hands, page 40	✓								★	
Emotions Song, page 140	✓	✓					★			
Excuse Me Photo Cube, page 114		✓	☆	☆						★
Excusing Tin with Tickets, page 74		✓								★
Feathery Finger Puppet, page 32	✓			☆	☆	☆	★		☆	☆
Feel the Mitten, page 25	✓	✓			★		☆		☆	
Feely Cube, page 75	✓				☆		☆		☆	★

★—Indicates Primary Activity
☆—Indicates Secondary Activity

Activity Name	Toddlers	Kids with Special Needs	Routine Changes	Settlers	Attention Grabbers	Stretchers	Extenders	Magic Carpet Activities	Magical Moments	Excusers
Felt-and-Velcro Hoop, page 96	✓	✓					★	☆		☆
Foam Guitar, page 80			★							
Folder of Flowers, page 146								★		
Follow the Light, page 119	✓	✓	★	☆						
Fox, Fox in a Box, page 61				☆	☆		★			
Get Your Wiggles Out, page 95						★	☆			
Giant Bubble, page 54				☆	★					
Gigantic Letters, page 122		✓		★						☆
Glove Clackers and Ringers, page 30	✓	✓				★				
Glow-in-the-Dark Bottle, page 52				☆	★			☆		
Glow-in-the-Dark Megaphone, page 118		✓	★							☆
Hands-On Necklace, page 38	✓								★	
Handy Glove Beanbag, page 28		✓		☆		★	☆	☆	☆	☆
Hanky Baby, page 124		✓		★						
Helping Hands, page 16		✓	★							
How Many Fingers?, page 39		✓					☆		★	☆
I Spy You, page 107									★	
It's All in the Hands, page 31		✓	☆				★	☆	☆	☆
Junk Box, page 72							☆		★	
Let Me Hand It to You, page 44		✓	☆	☆						★
Let's Wave Good-Bye, page 41	✓			☆						★
Lunch Box, page 60							★			
Magic Glove Wand, page 14		✓	★	☆	☆	☆	☆		☆	
Magic Mitt, page 34	✓						★	☆	☆	
Magic Pickup Lotion, page 19	✓	✓	★	☆						
Magnetic Board with Pieces, page 105								★		
Magnetic Fingertips, page 36		✓						★		
Message Box, page 163	✓				★		☆			
Mini Sound Shakers, page 149		✓				☆		★		☆
Mini Microphone, page 154	✓	✓							★	
Mirroring, page 131			☆			★				
Mixing Oil and Water, page 69	✓	✓						★		
Move-Your-Body Cube, page 136	✓	✓					★			☆
Music Box Dancer, page 57			☆			★			☆	☆
Musical 3-D Shapes, page 166	✓	✓				★				

★—Indicates Primary Activity
☆—Indicates Secondary Activity

Activity Name	Toddlers	Kids with Special Needs	Routine Changes	Settlers	Attention Grabbers	Stretchers	Extenders	Magic Carpet Activities	Magical Moments	Excusers
Musical Pictures, page 152	✓	✓							★	
Names on Notepads, page 176	✓	✓				☆	☆		☆	★
Name-That-Shape Mat, page 162	✓			★						
Our-Favorite-Songs Bag, page 59	✓						★		☆	
Pass the Beanbag, page 120		✓	★							☆
Pass the Shape, page 177		✓	☆							★
Patterns with Hands, page 24				★			☆		☆	
Peek-a-Boo and Pop-Up Cards, page 110							☆		★	☆
Pencil and Stencil Box, page 64		✓						★		
Photo Key Chains, page 88	✓			★				☆		
Pick-a-Card Exercises, page 29	✓					★				
Picking Up Shapes, page 174	✓	✓							★	
Pickup Message Bag, page 49			★							
Pictorial Schedules, page 86		✓	★							
Place-Mat Puzzles, page 104	✓	✓						★		
Place Mat Sit-Upons, page 89		✓		★						
Pom-Pom Cube, page 65	✓							★		
Puppy and Kitty Box, page 66		✓					☆	★		
Quiet-As-a-Mouse Puppet, page 112			☆						☆	★
Scrubber Puzzles, page 141	✓	✓					☆	★		
See-Through Bag, page 53					★				☆	
See-Through Crayons, page 151	✓	✓							★	
Sensory Soothers, page 125	✓	✓		★						
Sensory-Sensitive Wands, page 82	✓	✓	★							
Shaker Bottles, page 58		✓				★				
Shape Matching, page 160		✓	★							
Shape Photo Book, page 167	✓	✓					★	☆		
Shape Stickers, page 161	✓	✓		★						☆
Shape-Matching Cards, page 172								★		
Shape-Up Aerobics, page 134		✓				★				
Shimmering Cloth, page 92	✓	✓			★					
Sing-a-Song Board, page 101								★	☆	
Smile Sticks, page 126	✓	✓			★					
Sock Animal Puppets, page 18	✓	✓	★		☆					☆
Song-Riddles, page 123	✓	✓		★			☆			☆

★—Indicates Primary Activity
☆—Indicates Secondary Activity

Activity Name

Activity Name	Toddlers	Kids with Special Needs	Routine Changes	Settlers	Attention Grabbers	Stretchers	Extenders	Magic Carpet Activities	Magical Moments	Excusers
Sponge Balls, page 129	✓	✓		☆	☆	★				
Sticker Match, page 106	✓	✓						★	☆	
Stickie Cube, page 93					★		☆			
Story Prop Box, page 102							★			
Streamers on a Hoop, page 132	✓					★				
Stuffed Animal Wand, page 128	✓	✓			★					
Styrofoam-Bead Bottles, page 68		✓						★		
Surprise Box, page 164	✓	✓			★					
Take My Hand, page 21	✓		☆	★		☆				☆
Teacher Pockets, page 150	✓	✓					☆		★	
"Toddlers Like To" Book, page 135	✓						★	☆	☆	
Treasure Bottle, page 50				★						
Tub of Snakes, page 90	✓			☆	★			☆		
Tube Roller, page 130	✓					★				
TV in a Box, page 62					☆		★	☆		
Twirling Ribbon Wand, page 156	✓	✓		☆	☆	☆	☆			★
Unique Handprints, page 22		✓		★		☆	☆		☆	☆
Velcro Bag with Photos, page 76		✓								★
Versatile Tri-Fold Board, page 98							★			
Wagon Box, page 48	✓		★							
Walk-Around Schedule Board, page 84		✓	★							
Water Pillows, page 145	✓							★		
Waving Shapes, page 165	✓	✓				★				☆
Weighted Fleece Bags, page 121		✓		★						
Whale Mat, page 87	✓			★						
What's in the Box?, page 51				★			☆			
What's in the Handbag?, page 27	✓			☆	★	☆	☆		☆	
Where Is the Animal?, page 139							★			
Who Has the Shape?, page 168	✓	✓	☆	☆			★			☆
Write-and-Wipe Cube, page 113										★